Le

**Faces i**

**Methuen Drama**

Published by Methuen Drama 2008

1 3 5 7 9 10 8 6 4 2

Methuen Drama
A & C Black Publishers Limited
36 Soho Square
London W1D 3QY
www.methuendrama.com

ISBN 978 1 408 11269 4

A CIP catalogue record for this book
is available from the British Library

Typeset by Country Setting, Kingsdown, Kent
Printed and bound in Great Britain by
CPI Cox & Wyman, Reading, RG1 8EX

### Caution

# ROYAL COURT

Royal Court Theatre presents

# FACES IN THE CROWD

by **Leo Butler**

First performance at the Royal Court Jerwood Theatre Upstairs, Sloane Square, London
on 18 October 2008.

# FACES IN THE CROWD

by **Leo Butler**

Joanne **Amanda Drew**
Dave **Con O'Neill**

Director **Clare Lizzimore**
Designers **William Fricker, Rae Smith**
Lighting Designer **Johanna Town**
Sound Designer **Emma Laxton**
Casting Director **Amy Ball**
Production Manager **Tariq Sayyid Rifaat**
Stage Managers **Nicola Chisholm, Ruth Murfitt**
Costume Supervisor **Jackie Orton**
Stage Management Work Placement **Fiona McCulloch**
Voice Coach **Sally Hague**

# THE COMPANY

## LEO BUTLER (Writer)

FOR THE ROYAL COURT: Airbag, Lucky Dog, Made of Stone, Redundant.

OTHER THEATRE INCLUDES: I'll Be The Devil (RSC/Tricycle); The Early Bird (Ransom Productions); Heroes (National Theatre Education); Devotion (Theatre Centre).

TELEVISION INCLUDES: Jerusalem the Golden (BBC Four/Fictionlab).

AWARDS INCLUDE: George Devine Award 2001 for Redundant; Peggy Ramsay Award for Individual Writing 1999 & 2008.

Leo is Writers' Tutor for the Royal Court's Young Writers' Programme.

## AMANDA DREW (Joanne)

FOR THE ROYAL COURT: The Ugly One, Mr Kolpert, The Man of Mode (& Out of Joint), The Libertine (& Out of Joint).

OTHER THEATRE INCLUDES: Chain Play, Enemies, Dona Rosita the Spinster (Almeida); Otherwise Engaged (Criterion); Play (BAC); Blithe Spirit (Theatre Royal Bath); Damages (Bush); 100 (The Imaginary Body); Madame Bovary, The House of Bernarda Alba (Shared Experience); Eastwood Ho!, The Malcontent, The Roman Actor (RSC/West End); The Memory of Water, Jubilee, Love in a Wood (RSC); Top Girls (New Vic); The School of Night (Minerva); Pericles (RNTS); Taking Sides (Manchester Library); John Gabriel Borkman, The Way of the World, Hove (National); The Good Times are Coming (Old Red Lion).

TELEVISION INCLUDES: Holby Blue, East Enders, Golden Hour, The Bill, No Angels, MIT, Men Behaving Badly, Tough Love, Paul Calfes Video Diary, Soldier Soldier, Between the Lines, Full Stretch, Degrees of Error, The Maitlands.

FILM INCLUDES: The Other Man.

AWARDS INCLUDE: 2003 Clarence Derwent Award for Eastward Ho!.

## WILLIAM FRICKER (Designer)

THEATRE INCLUDES: Sleeping Beauty (Margate Theatre Royal); Much Ado About Nothing (Redshift Theatre Co.); The Lion The Witch and The Wardrobe, Cider with Rosie, The Good Person of Szechuan, Kes, Burn, 17 (Salisbury Playhouse); Godspell, The Ballad of Elizabeth Sulky Mouth (Greenwich); Todd (Kabosh Theatre/Old Museum Arts Centre); Pleasure and Pain (Citizens, Glasgow); Women Beware Women, Bacchae/Back-up (Allardyce Niccoll Studio); Coriolanus (Crescent); York Cycle (University of Toronto).

DANCE INCLUDES: What Planet are you Living On? (Mind the Gap Dance Theatre/tour); Hothouse (Topiary Dance).

# EMMA LAXTON (Sound Designer)

FOR THE ROYAL COURT: That Face (& Duke of York's), Gone Too Far!, Catch, Scenes From The Back Of Beyond, Woman and Scarecrow, The World's Biggest Diamond, Incomplete and Random Acts of Kindness, My Name Is Rachel Corrie (& Playhouse/Minetta Lane, New York/Galway Festival/Edinburgh Festival), Bone, The Weather, Bear Hug, Terrorism, Food Chain.

OTHER THEATRE INCLUDES: Welcome to Ramallah (iceandfire); Pornography (Birmingham Rep/Traverse); 2000 Feet Away, Tinderbox (Bush); Shoot/Get Treasure/Repeat (National); Europe (Dundee Rep/Barbican Pit); Other Hands (Soho); The Unthinkable (Sheffield); My Dad's a Birdman (Young Vic); The Gods Are Not To Blame (Arcola); Late Fragment (Tristan Bates).

# CLARE LIZZIMORE (Director)

FOR THE ROYAL COURT: War & Peace/Fear & Misery (Latitude Festival); The Mother (co-directed with MaxStafford-Clark); Talking Dirty (Rough Cut).

OTHER THEATRE AS DIRECTOR INCLUDES: On the Rocks (Hampstead); Jonah and Otto (Manchester Royal Exchange Studio); Tom Fool (Citizens, Glasgow/Bush); Sky High and After That: Gorbals Voices, Lazy Days, Memorial (Citizens, Glasgow); She Bursts into Flames, Murder in the Red Barn, The Most Humane Way to Kill a Lobster (Theatre 503); This One's For You Hula Girl, I Don't Want to Grow Up (Old Vic New Voices 24 Hour Plays).

OTHER THEATRE AS ASSISTANT DIRECTOR INCLUDES: Women of Troy, The Hothouse (National); Henry VIII (RSC); Romeo & Juliet, Blood Wedding, Charlotte's Web, Whatever Happened to Baby Jane? (Citizens, Glasgow); 24 Hour Plays (Old Vic); 270° (Paines Plough/Young Vic); As You Like It (Sphinx Theatre Co. tour).

# CON O'NEILL (Dave)

THEATRE INCLUDES: The Female of the Species (Vaudeville); The Caretaker (Sheffield/Tricycle); Midnight Cowboy (Assembly, Edinburgh); Southwark Fair, Mother Clap's Molly House, Blasted (National); Telstar (No. 1 tour/West End); Featuring Loretta, The Fastest Clock, The Awakening (Hampstead); Woyzeck (Hull Truck); Blood Brothers (West End/Broadway); Ridley Walker (Royal Exchange).

TELEVISION INCLUDES: Criminal Justice, Learners, The Stepfather, My Hero, Ultimate Force, Murder Squad, The Illustrated Mum, In Deep, Trial and Retribution, Waking the Dead, Real Women, Always and Everyone, Cider With Rosie, Heartbeat, Macbeth, Tom Jones, Wycliffe, Peak Practice, Soldier Soldier, Moving Story, Inspector Morse, Casualty, Pie in the Sky, The Riff Raff Element, Amongst Barbarians, One Summer, Norbert Smith.

FILM INCLUDES: Telstar, What's Your Name 41?, The Last Seduction, Bedrooms and Hallways, A Perfect Match, Three Steps to Heaven, Scarborough Ahoy!, The Lilac Bus, Dancin' Thru the Dark.

AWARDS INCLUDE: Olivier Award for Blood Brothers 1988.

# RAE SMITH (Designer)

FOR THE ROYAL COURT: Shining City (also Dublin), Dublin Carol, The Weir (also West End/Broadway/World tour), Presence, Some Voices, Trust.

OTHER THEATRE INCLUDES: War Horse, St Joan, A Pillar of the Community (National); The Seafarer (National/ Broadway) The Street of Crocodiles (National/ Complicité/West End); An Ideal Husband (Abbey/Dublin); Pedro the Great Pretender, As You Like It, (RSC/West End); Oliver Twist (with American Rep Theatre/Broadway/San Francisco); Juno and the Paycock (Donmar/ New York); Cyrano, Way of the World, Charley's Aunt (Manchester Royal Exchange).

OPERA INCLUDES: Das Rheingold, Die Walküre, (Opéra National du Rhin); Bird of Night (Royal Opera House Linbury); Don Giovanni ( Welsh National Opera); The Magic Flute (Opera North and Garsington).

AWARDS INCLUDE: Olivier Award for War Horse 2008; Evening Standard Award for War Horse; 2007; OBIE for Oliver Twist 2007.

# JOHANNA TOWN (Lighting Designer)

FOR THE ROYAL COURT: Over 50 productions, including Rhinoceros, My Child, Scenes From The Back Of Beyond, My Name is Rachel Corrie (& West End/Galway Festival/Edinburgh Festival/Minetta Lane, New York), Rainbow Kiss, The Winterling, The Woman Before, Way To Heaven, A Girl in a Car With a Man, Under the Whaleback, The Kitchen, O Go My Man (with Out of Joint), Talking to Terrorists (with Out of Joint), Shopping and Fucking (with Out of Joint/West End), The Steward of Christendom (with Out of Joint/Broadway).

OTHER THEATRE INCLUDES: The Glass Menagerie (Manchester Royal Exchange/Theatre Royal Bath tour); Fat Pig (Trafalgar Studios); The Tragedy of Thomas Hobbes (RSC); Small Craft Warnings (Arcola); Guantanamo (Tricycle/West End/New York); Rose (National/New York); Arabian Nights, Our Lady of Sligo (New York); Little Malcolm and His Struggle Against the Eunuchs (West End/Hampstead); Feelgood, Top Girls, Via Dolorosa, Beautiful Thing (West End); The Triumph of Love, All the Ordinary Angels (Royal Exchange); To Kill A Mockingbird (Birmingham Rep/tour); The Glassroom (Hampstead); King of Hearts (Out of Joint/Hampstead); The Overwhelming, The Permanent Way, She Stoops to Conquer (Out of Joint/National); Macbeth (Out of Joint world tour); In Praise of Love (Chichester); Dead Funny (West Yorkshire Playhouse); How Love is Spelt (Bush); I.D. (Almeida/BBC3); Badnuff (Soho); The Dumb Waiter (Oxford).

OPERA INCLUDES: The Secret Marriage, Cinderella (Scottish Opera); The Marriage of Figaro (Classical Opera Company); Tobias and the Angel (Almeida Opera Festival); The Marriage of Figaro, Otello (Nice Opera House); The Marriage of Figaro, The Merry Widow, Eugene Onegin, The Abduction from Seraglio (Opera 80); Die Fledermaus, La Boheme, La Traviata, The Magic Flute, The Poisoned Chalice (Music Theatre London).

# THE ENGLISH STAGE COMPANY
# AT THE ROYAL COURT

*'For me the theatre is really a religion or way of life.
You must decide what you feel the world is about and
what you want to say about it, so that everything in
the theatre you work in is saying the same thing ...
A theatre must have a recognisable attitude. It will
have one, whether you like it or not.'*

George Devine, first artistic director of the
English Stage Company: notes for an unwritten
book.

photo: Stephen Cummiskey

As Britain's leading national company dedicated to new work, the Royal Court Theatre produces new plays
of the highest quality, working with writers from all backgrounds, and addressing the problems and
possibilities of our time.

"The Royal Court has been at the centre of British cultural life for the past 50 years, an engine room for
new writing and constantly transforming the theatrical culture" Stephen Daldry

Since its foundation in 1956, the Royal Court has presented premieres by almost every leading
contemporary British playwright, from John Osborne's *Look Back in Anger* to Caryl Churchill's *A Number* and
Tom Stoppard's *Rock 'n' Roll*. Just some of the other writers to have chosen the Royal Court to premiere
their work include Edward Albee, John Arden, Samuel Beckett, Edward Bond, Jez Butterworth, Martin Crimp,
Ariel Dorfman, Christopher Hampton, David Hare, Eugène Ionesco, Ann Jellicoe, Terry Johnson, Sarah Kane,
David Mamet, Martin McDonagh, Conor McPherson, Mark Ravenhill, Wole Soyinka, Polly Stenham,
David Storey, debbie tucker green, Arnold Wesker and Roy Williams.

"It is risky to miss a production there" Financial Times

In addition to its full-scale productions, the Royal Court also facilitates international work at a grass roots
level, developing exchanges which bring young writers to Britain and sending British writers, actors and
directors to work with artists around the world. The Royal Court Young Writers' Programme also works to
develop new voices with their bi-annual Festival and year-round development work for writers under the
age of 26.

"Yes, the Royal Court is on a roll. Yes, Dominic Cooke has just the genius and kick that this venue needs...
It's fist-bitingly exciting." Independent

20 Nov 2008 – 10 Jan 2009

JERWOOD THEATRE DOWNSTAIRS

ROYAL COURT

# wig out!

## by Tarell Alvin McCraney

Bringing to glorious, vivid life, a riotous, defiant drag queen subculture.

Online Media Partner

gaydarnation.com

Print Media Partner

attitude

# PROGRAMME SUPPORTERS

The Royal Court (English Stage Company Ltd) receives its principal funding from Arts Council England, London. It is also supported financially by a wide range of private companies, charitable and public bodies, and earns the remainder of its income from the box office and its own trading activities.

The Genesis Foundation supports the Royal Court's work with International Playwrights.

The Jerwood Charity supports new plays by new playwrights through the Jerwood New Playwrights series.

The Artistic Director's Chair is supported by a lead grant from The Peter Jay Sharp Foundation, contributing to the activities of the Artistic Director's office. Over the past ten years the BBC has supported the Gerald Chapman Fund for directors.

## ROYAL COURT DEVELOPMENT ADVOCATES
John Ayton
Anthony Burton
Sindy Caplan (Vice Chair)
Cas Donald
Allie Esiri
Celeste Fenichel
Stephen Marquardt
Emma Marsh
Mark Robinson
William Russell (Chair)

## PUBLIC FUNDING
Arts Council England, London
British Council
London Challenge

## CHARITABLE DONATIONS
American Friends of the Royal Court Theatre
Bulldog Prinsep Theatrical Fund
Gerald Chapman Fund
Columbia Foundation
The Sidney & Elizabeth Corob Charitable Trust
Cowley Charitable Trust
The Edmond de Rothschild Foundation*
The Dorset Foundation
The D'oyly Carte Charitable Trust
E*TRADE Financial
Esmée Fairbairn Foundation
The Edwin Fox Foundation
Francis Finlay*
The Garfield Weston Foundation
Genesis Foundation
Haberdashers' Company
Jerwood Charitable Foundation
John Thaw Foundation
Kudos Film and Televisoin
Lloyds TSB Foundation for England and Wales
Dorothy Loudon Foundation*

Lynn Foundation
John Lyon's Charity
The Laura Pels Foundation*
The Martin Bowley Charitable Trust
Paul Hamlyn Foundation
The Peggy Ramsay Foundation
Quercus Charitable Trust
Jerome Robbins Foundation*
Rose Foundation
Royal College of Psychiatrists
The Royal Victoria Hall Foundation
The Peter Jay Sharp Foundation*
Sobell Foundation
Wates Foundation

## SPONSORS
BBC
Dom Perignon
Links of London
Pemberton Greenish
Smythson of Bond Street

## BUSINESS BENEFACTORS & MEMBERS
Grey London
Hugo Boss
Lazard
Merrill Lynch
Vanity Fair

## INDIVIDUAL SUPPORTERS

### ICE-BREAKERS
Act IV
Anonymous
Ossi and Paul Burger
Mrs Helena Butler
Cynthia Corbett
Shantelle David
Charlotte & Nick Fraser
Mark & Rebecca Goldbart
Linda Grosse
Mr & Mrs Tim Harvey-Samuel
David Lanch
Colette & Peter Levy

Watcyn Lewis
David Marks
Nicola McFarland
Janet & Michael Orr
Pauline Pinder
Mr & Mrs William Poeton
The Really Useful Group
Lois Sieff OBE
Gail Steele
Nick & Louise Steidl

### GROUND-BREAKERS
Anonymous
Moira Andreae
Jane Attias*
Elizabeth & Adam Bandeen
Philip Blackwell
Mrs D H Brett
Sindy & Jonathan Caplan
Mr & Mrs Gavin Casey
Carole & Neville Conrad
Clyde Cooper
Andrew & Amanda Cryer
Robyn M Durie
Hugo Eddis
Mrs Margaret Exley CBE
Robert & Sarah Fairbairn
Celeste & Peter Fenichel
Andrew & Jane Fenwick
Ginny Finegold
Wendy Fisher
Hugh & Henri Fitzwilliam-Lay
Joachim Fleury
Lydia & Manfred Gorvy
Richard & Marcia Grand*
Nick & Catherine Hanbury-Williams
Sam & Caroline Haubold
Nicholas Josefowitz
David P Kaskel &
Christopher A Teano
Peter & Maria Kellner*
Mrs Joan Kingsley &
Mr Philip Kingsley
Mr & Mrs Pawel Kisielewski
Varian Ayers and Gary Knisely
Kathryn Ludlow
Emma Marsh

Barbara Minto
Gavin & Ann Neath
Mark Robinson
Paul & Jill Ruddock
William & Hilary Russell
Jenny Sheridan
Anthony Simpson & Susan Boster
Brian D Smith
Carl & Martha Tack
Katherine & Michael Yates

### BOUNDARY-BREAKERS
John and Annoushka Ayton
Katie Bradford
Tim Fosberry
Edna & Peter Goldstein
Reade and Elizabeth Griffith
Sue & Don Guiney
Rosanna Laurence
Jan and Michael Topham

### MOVER-SHAKERS
Anonymous
Dianne & Michael Bienes*
Lois Cox
Cas & Philip Donald
John Garfield
Duncan Matthews QC

### HISTORY-MAKERS
Jack & Linda Keenan*
Miles Morland
Ian & Carol Sellars

### MAJOR DONORS
Daniel & Joanna Friel
Deborah & Stephen Marquardt
Lady Sainsbury of Turville
NoraLee & Jon Sedmak*

*Supporters of the American Friends of the Royal Court

# FOR THE ROYAL COURT

Royal Court Theatre, Sloane Square, London SW1W 8AS
Tel: 020 7565 5050 Fax: 020 7565 5001
info@royalcourttheatre.com, www.royalcourttheatre.com

Artistic Director **Dominic Cooke**
Associate Directors **Ramin Gray\*, Sacha Wares**[+]
Artistic Associate **Emily McLaughlin**
Associate Producer **Diane Borger**
Diversity Associate **Ola Animashawun\***
Education Associate **Lynne Gagliano\***
Trainee Director (ITV Scheme) **Natalie Ibu**[‡]

Literary Manager **Ruth Little**
Literary Associate **Terry Johnson\***
Senior Reader **Nicola Wass**
Pearson Playwright **Daniel Jackson**[†]
Literary Assistant **Marcelo Dos Santos**

Associate Director International **Elyse Dodgson**
International Administrator **Chris James**
International Assistant **William Drew**

YWP Manager **Nina Lyndon**
Writers' Tutor **Leo Butler\***

Casting Director **Amy Ball**
Casting Assistant **Lotte Hines**

Head of Production **Paul Handley**
JTU Production Manager **Tariq Rifaat**
Production Assistant **Sarah Davies**
Head of Lighting **Matt Drury**
Lighting Deputy **Nicki Brown**
Lighting Assistants **Stephen Andrews, Katie Pitt**
Head of Stage **Steven Stickler**
Stage Deputy **Duncan Russell**
Stage Chargehand **Lee Crimmen**
Chargehand Carpenter **Richard Martin**
Head of Sound **Ian Dickinson**
Sound Deputy **David McSeveney**
Head of Costume **Iona Kenrick**
Costume Deputy **Jackie Orton**
Wardrobe Assistant **Pam Anson**

Executive Director **Kate Horton**
Head of Finance and Administration **Helen Perryer**
Planning Administrator **Davina Shah**
Senior Finance and Administration Officer **Martin Wheeler**
Finance Officer **Rachel Harrison\***
Finance and Administration Assistant **Tessa Rivers**

Head of Communications **Kym Bartlett**
Marketing Manager **Becky Wootton**
Press Officer **Stephen Pidcock**
Audience Development Officer **Gemma Frayne**

Sales Manager **Kevin West**
Deputy Sales Manager **Daniel Alicandro**
Box Office Sales Assistants **Shane Hough, Ciara O'Toole**

Head of Development **Jenny Mercer**
Development Manager **Hannah Clifford**
Development Officer **Lucy James**
Development Assistant **Penny Saward**

Theatre Manager **Bobbie Stokes**
Front of House Manager **Claire Simpson**
Deputy Theatre Manager **Daniel O'Neill**
Duty Manager **Stuart Grey\***
Deputy Bar and Food Manager **Paul Carstairs**
Bookshop Manager **Simon David**
Assistant Bookshop Manager **Edin Suljic\***
Bookshop Assistant **Emily Lucienne**
Building Maintenance Administrator **Jon Hunter**
Stage Door/Reception **Simon David\*, Paul Lovegrove, Tyrone Lucas**

Thanks to all of our box office assistants, ushers and bar staff.

+ Sacha Wares' post is supported by the BBC through the Gerald Chapman Fund.

‡ The post of Trainee Director is supported by ITV under the ITV Theatre Director Scheme.

† This theatre has the support of the Pearson Playwrights' scheme, sponsor the Peggy Ramsay Foundation.

\* Part-time.

## ENGLISH STAGE COMPANY

President
**Sir John Mortimer CBE QC**

Vice President
**Dame Joan Plowright CBE**

Honorary Council
**Sir Richard Eyre CBE**
**Alan Grieve CBE**
**Martin Paisner CBE**

Council
Chairman **Anthony Burton**
Vice Chairman **Graham Devlin**

Members
**Jennette Arnold**
**Judy Daish**
**Sir David Green KCMG**
**Joyce Hytner OBE**
**Stephen Jeffreys**
**Phyllida Lloyd**
**James Midgley**
**Sophie Okonedo**
**Alan Rickman**
**Anita Scott**
**Katharine Viner**
**Stewart Wood**

## Acknowledgements

I'd like to thank Ruth Little, Dominic Cooke, and Clare Lizzimore for all their encouragement and guidance in the writing of this play.

I'd also like to thank Howard Gooding, the Peggy Ramsay Foundation and, as always, Nazzi and Beatrice.

# Faces in the Crowd

## Characters

**Dave**, *forty-four years old*
**Joanne**, *thirty-nine years old*

Both are originally from Sheffield, South Yorkshire.

## Setting

Dave's studio flat, east London.

The building is situated in Shoreditch, sandwiched between Bishopsgate, Hoxton and Bethnal Green.

The building is made up of offices on the ground floor and, above them, three studio flats.

Dave's flat is the middle one – Flat B.

The flat comprises three separate spaces.

The living space, which includes: a kitchen area (counter/ stools/cooker/hob/cupboards/fridge); an office area (desk/ laptop/files/junk) by the window (with blinds); and, in the centre, a 'living area' including a futon, a plasma-screen TV and a small armchair.

The bathroom (toilet, sink, cabinet, bath/shower unit).

The bedroom. Like the living space, the bedroom has its own window (with blinds), looking out onto the street below and the ex-council flats opposite. There is a king-size bed, a bedside cabinet, a chest of drawers, etc.

Three doors.

The rest of the furniture and interior decoration is made obvious in the text.

## Notes on the Text

. . . denotes a trailing off, and is usually followed by a pause.

. . . within a passage of dialogue denotes a trailing off, that is quickly interrupted.

. . . – denotes a clear interruption.

*Studio flat, east London.*
*Summer 2007. Night.*
*The windows and blinds are shut.*
**Dave** *is with* **Joanne**.
**Joanne** *has just arrived, standing close by the door. She carries her large brown handbag and wears casual clothes.*
**Dave** *is in his work suit.*

*Long pause.*

**Dave**    Did yer find it alright?

**Joanne**    Just about.

*Pause.*

**Dave**    Sorry.

**Joanne**    What?

**Dave**    Should've come and met yer shunt I? Off the tube, I mean.

**Joanne**    It weren't far.

**Dave**    No, but . . .

*Pause.*

This area.

**Joanne**    Yeah, I noticed.

**Dave**    Not as bad as it looks.

**Joanne**    Int it?

**Dave**    There's people spend a fortune to live round 'ere. Yer could buy a three-bedroom house back home f'what yer'd pay for one of these.

**Joanne**    That's London for yer then int it?

**Dave**    Yeah.

*Pause.*

Yeah it is.

**Joanne**   I like it.

**Dave**   D'yer?

**Joanne**   It's nice.

**Dave**   Oh . . .

**Joanne**   Self-contained.

**Dave**   Oh, well . . .

**Joanne**   Better than I expected anyway.

**Dave**   Thanks.

*Over the following,* **Joanne** *snoops round the flat.*

*Long pause.*

**Joanne**   Don't mind me havin' a nose d'yer?

*Long pause.*

This all yours?

**Dave**   What?

**Joanne**   The furniture. This all your doin'?

**Dave**   Partly.

**Joanne**   I see.

**Dave**   He owns the whole building.

**Joanne**   Who?

**Dave**   The landlord. I work with 'is brother.

**Joanne**   Oh, right.

**Dave**   We've become sort of friends. On and off. At work, I mean. It's him who put us on to this.

**Joanne**   Good of 'im.

**Dave**   It's only temporary. He's away with the navy. Marcus, I mean – that's the landlord. He's stationed down Southampton f'the rest of the year.

**Joanne**  Landed on yer feet then 'ant yer?

**Dave**  Well, it'll do like.

**Joanne**  Minimalist.

*Pause.*

That is what they call it, isn't it?

**Dave**  I wunt know, Joanne.

**Joanne**  Looks smaller from the outside.

**Dave**  Tardis.

**Joanne**  What?

**Dave**  Doctor Who's Tardis. That's what we call it.

*Pause.*

Yeah.

*Long pause.*

Though I was thinkin' of movin' further into Hackney.

*Pause.*

Further in . . .

**Joanne**  This the bathroom through 'ere?

**Dave**  Oh . . .

**Joanne** *opens the bathroom door and peers in.*

**Dave**  Yeah. Yeah, that's . . .

**Joanne**  Smells clean.

**Dave**  Thanks.

**Joanne**  Someone's got 'im trained.

**Dave**  I wouldn't go that far.

**Joanne**  Wunt yer?

**Dave**  I wouldn't, no.

**Joanne** *switches the light on and steps inside.*

*Pause.*

**Joanne**   D'yer mind if I . . . ?

**Dave**   No, you . . .

**Joanne** *shuts the bathroom door.*

**Dave**   Don't mind me.

*Long pause.*

**Joanne** *goes to the toilet.*
*Once finished, she flushes and moves to the bathroom sink.*
*She washes her hands, filling up the sink with water.*

*Pause.*

**Joanne** *proceeds to wash her face, washing her make-up off.*
*Once done, she dries her face with a towel and checks her reflection.*

*She opens the bathroom cabinet and snoops around inside.*
*She examines, among other things, a box of tampons, and a tube of
Canesten cream.*

*As she is doing all this,* **Dave***, in the other room, hesitates.*

*Pause.*

**Dave** *moves to the kitchen area, removes a bottle of white wine from the
fridge and takes two wine glasses from the cupboard.*
*He is about to open the bottle of wine when his mobile phone starts
ringing.*
*He rushes to find the mobile phone.*
*He finds the mobile phone, which is in the pocket of his suit jacket, draped
over one of the kitchen stools.*
*He takes the mobile phone, presses the 'busy' button.*
*The mobile phone stops ringing.*
*He turns the mobile phone onto silent, then pockets it.*

*He hesitates.*

*Pause.*

*He moves to the window.*

*He looks out of the window.*
*He shuts the window and pulls the blinds down.*
*He unbuttons the top button of his shirt.*
*He turns the fan on.*
*He hesitates.*

*Pause.*

*He takes the mobile phone out of his pocket.*
*He presses a couple of buttons, then puts the phone to his ear and listens to a voice message.*

*As he listens, he tidies up the papers on his work desk.*
*He then spots a pair of tracksuit bottoms and a T-shirt on the futon.*
*He grabs them both and looks for somewhere to put them.*

*He turns off the mobile phone and puts it in his pocket.*
*He enters the bedroom, and throws the tracksuit bottoms and T-shirt under the bed.*

*He re-enters the central living space.*

**Joanne** *re-enters, turning the bathroom light off and shutting the door.*

**Joanne**   Cosy.

**Dave**   Well, like I say . . .

**Joanne**   Yer lookin' after it for 'im.

**Dave**   It's not cheap.

**Joanne**   It doesn't look cheap.

**Dave**   Should've seen the dump I was in before.

*Over the next,* **Joanne** *makes herself at home. She moves to the kitchen area and puts her handbag down on one of the chairs. She takes her cigarettes from her jacket, then takes her jacket off, draping it over one of the stools. She sits on the stool.*

**Dave** *follows her to the kitchen area and proceeds to open the bottle of wine and pour two glasses.*

**Dave**   Over the river, over in Peckham. This is what, comin' up five year back now? Used t' take me about two hours just t' get to n' from work every day.

**Joanne**   Must've took its toll.

**Dave**   Bloody shoebox.

**Joanne**   Weren't yer knackered?

**Dave**   That's what I mean.

**Joanne**   I'm knackered just gettin' through King's Cross in one piece.

**Dave**   Good journey was it?

**Joanne**   What?

**Dave**   The train.

**Joanne**   I suppose so, yeah.

**Dave**   Yer weren't held up or anything?

**Joanne**   Straight through.

**Dave**   That's good then int it?

**Joanne**   Stopped once at Chesterfield. Once again at Leicester.

**Dave**   Good, yeah.

**Joanne**   Luton then 'ere.

**Dave**   Right.

**Joanne**   St Pancras.

**Dave**   No, that's good, Joanne.

**Joanne**   Tube all the way to Old Street.

**Dave**   Beats the bloody coach dunt it?

**Joanne**   By about four hour, yeah.

*She sparks a cigarette.*
*Long pause.*

Yer accent's gone.

**Dave**   Has it?

**Joanne**   Yer don't sound like you.

*Long pause.*

**Dave** *opens one of the cupboards and fetches* **Joanne** *an ashtray, which he places on the side.*

**Dave**   I was livin' in Plumstead before then. Before Peckham, that is.

**Joanne**   Where?

**Dave**   House share. Me n' a bunch of ex-grads. Fuckin' . . .

*He hands* **Joanne** *her glass of wine.*

*Pause.*

**Dave**   Yeah.

**Joanne**   Moved about a bit then, yeah?

**Dave**   'Ere n' there. Yer know. Get me bearings.

**Joanne**   Took its toll I see.

**Dave**   What?

**Joanne**   No wonder yer goin' bald.

**Dave**   Bald?

**Joanne**   Thought I'd got the wrong address for a minute.

*Pause.*

**Dave**   Oh . . .

**Joanne**   I'm jokin', yer prat, can't yer take a joke?

*With her wine and cigarette, she moves to the window and peers through the blinds.*

*Long pause.*

View's not up to much.

**Dave**   Sorry?

**Joanne**   Can't say it's too inspiring. The Texaco.

**Dave**    Yer can see the Gherkin during the day.

**Joanne**    I can see the what?

**Dave**    The Gherkin, yer know? Norman Foster.

**Joanne**    Weren't too taken wi' the homeless either. D'they always look like that?

**Dave**    Like what?

**Joanne**    Like they just stepped out o' Topshop.

**Dave**    'Ow d'yer mean?

**Joanne**    Bit trendy aren't they?

**Dave**    Are they?

**Joanne**    Brand-new pair o' trainers on the tramp.

**Dave**    'Oo?

**Joanne**    Beardy bollocks by the cashpoint there. 'Im n' 'is Alsation.

**Dave**    Yeah, he's always . . .

*Pause.*

He's somethin' of a fixture . . . –

**Joanne**    Gi'im a shave yer could stick 'im on a catwalk.

**Dave**    'Im or the dog?

**Joanne**    'E could give you a run f'yer money. (*Of* **Dave***'s shirt.*) What is that, Sainsbury's own?

**Dave**    Fuck off, it's Paul Smith.

**Joanne**    I'm surprised yer can put up with that noise.

*Pause.*

No offence.

**Dave**    None taken.

**Joanne**    Someone as sensitive as you. Thought yer'd be livin' in the woods or somert.

**Dave**    Oh no . . .

**Joanne**    You n' the muse. Yer still writing?

**Dave**    Not really.

**Joanne**    No?

**Dave**    No, nothing . . .

**Joanne** *moves to the office area and sits at* **Dave***'s desk, peering at the laptop screen and his papers.*

*Pause.*

**Dave**    Odds n' sods, yer know? Nothin' worth . . . −

**Joanne**    Nowt worth readin'.

**Dave**    No, not for . . . −

**Joanne**    Nothin' that's goin' t' set the world on fire.

**Dave**    Can't say I've really 'ad the time, Joanne.

**Joanne**    'Ant yer?

**Dave**    I haven't, no.

*Pause.*

No, not for years.

**Joanne**    I've got me own business now.

**Dave**    Okay.

**Joanne**    I've got me own little florist's, Dave, yeah.

**Dave**    Oh, right.

**Joanne** *digs in her pocket and pulls out a business card, which she offers to* **Dave***, who takes it.*

**Joanne**    Found a place up in Woodseats goin' f'sale. This is, what? Eighteen month back. Used t' be a kiddies' clothes shop.

**Dave**    Brilliant.

**Joanne**    It's me dad's doin' really. 'E stripped it all out, 'im n' our Phillip.

**Dave**   That's good of 'im.

**Joanne**   Well 'e's hardly goin' t' say no.

**Dave**   I always liked your brother.

**Joanne**   Mum's been helpin' out with all the day-to-day . . . yer know?

**Dave**   Doin' well f'yerself then, yeah?

**Joanne**   We're doin' alright, Dave, yeah. All things considerin'. Valentines, weddings, the odd funeral 'ere n' there.

**Dave**   Cashin' in on the dead.

**Joanne**   Got t' pay yer way somehow.

**Dave**   Got to, yeah.

*Pause.*

*He offers the business card back to* **Joanne***, who takes it.*

**Dave**   I like the little bumblebees.

**Joanne**   Always thought you'd end up on the best-seller list.

**Dave**   Yeah?

*Pause.*

Yeah, well . . .

**Joanne**   You and J. K. Rowling.

**Dave**   I don't really do that.

**Joanne**   Yer don't really make any money yer mean.

**Dave**   No, I don't really do prepubescent wizards.

**Joanne**   She's done very well out of it.

**Dave**   It's not about that though is it?

**Joanne**   Too busy savin' the planet.

**Dave**   Eh?

**Joanne**  Too busy savin' the orang-utans from extinction. Are you plannin' on goin' to Borneo?

**Dave**  Why would I want to go to Borneo?

**Joanne**  That's what it says here.

**Dave**  No, I'm . . . –

**Joanne**  The Orangutan Conservation Project.

**Dave**  I was just browsing a few sites, that's all.

**Joanne**  That's very noble of yer, Dave.

**Dave**  It's fascinatin' stuff really.

**Joanne**  Aren't they payin' you enough at that firm o' yours?

**Dave**  They're payin' me fine.

**Joanne**  Can't 'ave got much job satisfaction then can yer?

*She enters the bedroom, turning the light on.*

*Long pause.*

*She snoops round the bedroom.*

**Dave** *puts his wine down and moves out of the kitchen area.*

*He goes to the laptop. Unseen by* **Joanne**, *he saves and shuts down a program and half closes the laptop lid.*

**Joanne** *sits on the bed, snooping at the bits and pieces on the bedside table.*

**Dave** *retrieves his glass of wine and then moves to the bedroom, standing in the doorway.*

*Long pause.*

**Dave**  Yeah, that's . . . –

**Joanne**  Impressive.

**Dave**  Yeah.

**Joanne**  King size.

**Dave**   It's not mine.

**Joanne**   Int it?

**Dave**   No, it's . . . –

**Joanne**   Somert f' the ladies.

**Dave**   I think he fancies 'imself as a bit of a Lothario.

**Joanne**   I think he fancies 'imself, yer mean.

**Dave**   Those sheets could do with a clean.

**Joanne**   Could they?

**Dave**   No, I mean . . .

*Pause.*

The whole flat, I mean. I was thinkin' of payin' a cleaner.

**Joanne**   Oh, right.

**Dave**   Once a month or somert. Nowt fancy, just . . . – yer know?

**Joanne**   'Alf expected some crack 'ouse.

**Dave**   What?

**Joanne**   You n' a bunch of refugees. Iraqi freedom fighters or somert.

**Dave**   Well, it's hardly the Savoy.

**Joanne**   Shacked up wi' some Pole.

**Dave**   Who?

**Joanne**   You n' all the other immigrants. Scrappin' over fake passports.

**Dave**   Yeah, that's funny.

**Joanne**   Coked up t' the eye balls.

**Dave**   Chance'd be a fine thing.

**Joanne**   Is that a strip club next door?

**Dave**    It is, yeah.

**Joanne**    Classy.

**Dave**    Can I make you somethin' to eat?

**Joanne** *continues looking at the bits and pieces on the bedside cabinet.*

*Long pause.*

**Dave**    Thought yer might be hungry, Joanne, all that travellin'.

*Long pause.*

All that way, I mean.

**Joanne** *finds and removes a* Marie Claire *magazine.*

*Long pause.*

**Dave**    Joanne . . . –

**Joanne**    Where is she then?

**Dave**    Who?

**Joanne**    *Marie Claire.*

*Pause.*

*Marie Claire*, look.

**Dave**    Oh . . . –

**Joanne** *flicks through the copy of* Marie Claire.

**Dave**    Oh, that.

**Joanne**    Yer readin' this?

**Dave**    No, not . . . –

**Joanne**    Can't quite see it meself.

**Dave**    Not really.

**Joanne**    Even if it has got Angelina on the front.

**Dave**    Not if I can help it, no.

**Joanne** *flicks through the magazine.*

*Long pause.*

Give me somert t' read when I get back tonight. Slimmin' tips.

**Dave**   'Elp yerself, yeah.

**Joanne**   I've lost half a stone since Christmas.

**Dave**   'Ave yer?

**Joanne**   Been a right fatty-fat-fat me. Yer sure she won't mind?

**Dave**   I expect she'll manage.

**Joanne**   Does she even know I'm 'ere?

*Pause.*

I'm not bothered.

**Dave**   No, she's . . .

**Joanne**   Out the way.

**Dave**   Sorry?

**Joanne**   Yer've sent 'er on 'er merry way.

**Dave**   I don't follow.

*Pause.*

No, she's out with friends. She's . . . –

**Joanne**   She's not goin' t' come burstin' through that door?

**Dave**   It doesn't work like that.

**Joanne**   'Ow does it work?

*Pause.*

**Dave**   It's nothin' . . . –

**Joanne**   It's temporary.

**Dave**   Yeah.

*Pause.*

Yeah, it's one of the few buildings weren't hit by the Blitz.

**Joanne**  Oh, that's lucky.

**Dave**  Yer can see all the original fixtures n' fittings if yer look. Yer can see where they've partitioned it into flats.

**Joanne**  I expect this used to be one big bathroom or somert.

**Dave**  Yer can judge it by the stairwell, yeah. They've even built offices down in the basement.

**Joanne**  Pretty popular then, yeah?

**Dave**  Oh, yeah, there's about thirty-odd bars in this area alone.

**Joanne**  Really?

**Dave**  It's like fuckin' *Blade Runner* or somert at the weekend. What with the licensing hours.

**Joanne**  Keeping you up all night are they?

**Dave**  They're really trendy.

**Joanne**  Are they?

**Dave**  Photographers, artists. Yer get a lot of bands playing. Lot of students, I think.

**Joanne**  Right.

**Dave**  That and all yer City kids seein' in the weekend.

**Joanne**  Like you, yer mean.

**Dave**  The neighbours.

**Joanne**  Who?

**Dave**  The new neighbours, they've just moved in downstairs. Derek and Yan.

**Joanne**  Derek and who?

**Dave**  Yan. She's Chinese. They're on the first floor downstairs, they're very friendly.

**Joanne**  They sound it.

**Dave**  He works in publishing.

**Joanne**    Yer should sell 'im one of yer stories.

**Dave**    No, I helped 'em move their stuff in the other weekend. They're very young, I mean.

**Joanne**    That's good then.

**Dave**    Them and the arsehole upstairs.

**Joanne**    Who?

**Dave**    The arsehole lives above us.

**Joanne**    Oh, right.

**Dave**    Danny.

**Joanne**    And he's an arsehole is he?

**Dave**    He's like Bob the bloody Builder or somert. Pullin' up his floorboards at two in the morning.

**Joanne**    Must be annoying.

**Dave**    Playing his music at full blast. Depeche Mode.

**Joanne**    I wunt stand for it me.

**Dave**    He's only twenty-three or somert. Yer'd think he owned the fuckin' building. Him n' the thousand bastard construction firms rippin' up the neighbourhood f' the last twelve months n' all. Scaffoldin' towers left, right n' centre. Pneumatic drills at half past eight in the mornin'. Diggin' up the pavements ready f' the friggin' Olympics no one ever wants. It's like havin' knives driven into yer skull.

**Joanne**    Best get movin' then 'ant yer?

**Dave**    I intend to, yeah.

*Long pause.*

Once I'm . . . –

*Pause.*

Yer know?

**Joanne**    You n' yer girlfriend.

**Dave**   She's not my girlfriend.

**Joanne**   Could just say yer binned it then cunt yer?

**Dave**   What?

**Joanne**   Say yer bagged it up for recyclin' or somert. Doin' yer bit f 'the environment.

**Dave**   I don't think she's that type.

**Joanne**   What type?

**Dave**   The recyclin' type.

**Joanne**   Int she?

**Dave**   No. I don't think . . . −

**Joanne**   What type is she then?

**Dave**   It's not something we really talk about.

**Joanne**   Dunt she care about 'er carbon footprint?

**Dave**   Her what?

**Joanne**   Dunt she give much thought to her emissions?

**Dave**   Yer takin' the piss.

**Joanne**   I thought that's what people like you did.

**Dave**   People like who?

**Joanne**   'Ow old is she then?

**Dave**   What?

**Joanne**   All legal is it?

**Dave**   Don't be stupid . . .

**Joanne**   All legal and above board? − Don't worry, I've not come t' pass judgement.

**Dave**   Yer don't 'ave t' pass judgement, Joanne.

*Long pause.*

'Ere.

**Joanne**   What?

**Dave**   No, I'll . . .

*Long pause.*

**Joanne**   What?

**Dave**   No, that bus.

*Pause.*

That bus, yer know? The 26. The one they tried to bomb.

**Joanne**   What about it?

**Dave**   That were just round the corner from 'ere.

**Joanne**   Was it?

**Dave**   Literally. Just round the corner by the church. Yer'll see it when yer next go out.

**Joanne**   Oh.

**Dave**   Come back from work and there's fuckin' meat wagons everywhere.

**Joanne**   Fancy.

**Dave**   Everywhere's taped off. All the streets, the shops, the whole fuckin' parade round the back. One week after July the seventh, and there's me.

**Joanne**   There's you, Dave.

**Dave**   I mean it's worlds apart from owt . . .

*Pause.*

**Joanne**   From owt you've ever . . . ?

**Dave**   I mean, we're only five minutes walk from Bethnal Green. The mosque like, the community. George Galloway n' 'is big bloody mouth.

**Joanne**   Did yer see any bodies?

**Dave**   Sorry?

**Joanne**    Dead bodies. Did yer see any?

*Pause.*

**Dave**    What?

**Joanne**    Don't tell me yer dint look.

**Dave**    I don't think anyone were killed that day were they?

**Joanne**    Weren't they?

**Dave**    No. They weren't.

**Joanne**    Not much of a story then is it?

*Pause.*

**Dave**    I'm just sayin' aren't I? It's somethin' that happened.

**Joanne**    I'm impressed.

**Dave**    It's somethin' that happened to me.

*Pause.*

It's good t' see yer, I mean. I'm glad yer could make it.

**Joanne** *takes her shoes off.*

*Long pause.*

**Dave**    Yeah. Well I'll just . . .

**Joanne**    Yer know yer grandad's died.

**Dave**    Has he?

*Long pause.*

Yeah.

*Pause.*

Yeah, well, that's . . . –

**Joanne**    Emphysema.

*She hands her shoes to* **Dave**.

*Long pause.*

**Dave**   Okay.

**Joanne**   Yer'll have to ask yer mother f' the details.

**Dave**   Thanks.

**Joanne**   I'm sorry I don't . . .

*Pause.*

I don't really . . . –

**Dave**   No, yer alright, that's . . . –

**Joanne**   I haven't really kept in touch.

**Dave**   Course.

**Joanne**   I went t' the funeral. More out o' courtesy than anything else.

*Pause.*

Make up the numbers n' that.

**Dave**   Yeah.

**Joanne**   This is what, three year back?

**Dave**   'Ow long?

**Joanne**   Yer should ring 'er sometime. Yer mum, I mean. I've got 'er number in me phone if yer need it.

**Dave**   No, that's . . .

**Joanne**   Yer lucky she's not followed me down 'ere 'erself. Ringin' me at work every five minutes. Christ knows how she got my number, she's like somert off MI5 the way she behaves. I've been convinced she's 'ad me phone tapped all week, the bloody signal on it. – You spoke to 'er?

**Dave**   Not for years.

**Joanne**   'Ant yer?

**Dave**   No, I . . .

*Pause.*

I haven't really . . . –

**Joanne**   Me neither.

**Dave**   Not for decades it feels like.

**Joanne**   Sometimes bump into 'er in town.

**Dave**   Right.

**Joanne**   Food 'all at M n' S.

**Dave**   Okay.

**Joanne**   Strugglin' with 'er bags down Chapel Walk. Face on it like doom.

**Dave**   Yeah, that makes sense.

**Joanne**   Found 'er cryin' on the steps of the Crucible one time.

**Dave**   Did yer?

**Joanne**   During the snooker finals. Just after you left.

**Dave**   Oh.

**Joanne**   Just after you abandoned us, I mean.

*Pause.*

**Dave**   Oh, okay.

**Joanne**   In fucking floods she was. On 'er way t' the bus stop, on 'er way home.

**Dave**   Yeah, that's . . .

**Joanne**   I tried askin' 'er about it.

**Dave**   Good.

**Joanne**   I did try, Dave.

**Dave**   Well, she was probably upset . . . –

**Joanne**   Tore one of me earrings out, the bitch.

**Dave**   She what?

**Joanne**   Went ballistic, Dave, yeah. Kickin' n' screamin'.
Every name under the sun and more. Middle o' town like, on a
Saturday. Way 'ome from the match wi' our Phillip.

**Dave**   Oh . . .

**Joanne**   And there's her. Springin' up on me like a bloody
Rottweiler. Mouthin' off like it were me who drove yer away.

**Dave**   Oh, well . . .

**Joanne**   Like I'd buried you under the patio or somert, stupid
idiot. Denyin' her of fuckin' grandkids and I'm like 'What?'

**Dave**   Yer know how emotional she gets.

**Joanne**   Split me earlobe in two n' all.

**Dave**   Yeah?

*Pause.*

Yeah, that's . . . –

**Joanne**   That's somert what 'appened t' me, Dave.

*Long pause.*

Course, we can laugh about it now.

*Pause.*

At the funeral, I mean.

**Dave**   Great, yeah.

**Joanne**   We 'ad a right fuckin' scream about it, Dave, don't
look at me like that, it's true.

*She removes her tights.*

*Long pause.*

You alright?

*Long pause.*

Dave . . .

**Dave**   Why shunt I fucking be?

**Joanne**   Yer don't look it.

**Dave**   Why shouldn't I be alright?

*Pause.*

**Joanne**   Dave . . . –

**Dave**   I'm 'ere aren't I?

**Joanne**   I don't know what you fuckin' are.

**Dave**   Alright, just . . . –

**Joanne**   Yer like some fuckin' shadow or somethin'.

**Dave**   Okay.

*Pause.*

Okay, yeah . . .

**Joanne**   No offence.

**Dave**   No, that's fair.

**Joanne**   Yer like some ghost, Dave.

**Dave**   We should probably eat somethin' then shouldn't we?

**Joanne**   We should what?

**Dave**   Let me cook yer somethin' at least.

**Joanne**   I 'ad a sandwich on the train.

**Dave**   Chorizo salad.

**Joanne**   What?

**Dave**   Chorizo and cannellini-bean salad.

**Joanne**   Are you takin' the piss?

**Dave**   No, it was in the *Guardian* last weekend.

**Joanne**   Since when did you read the *Guardian*?

**Dave**   No, I thought I might . . .

**Joanne**   Sorry, I shouldn't laugh.

**Dave**   Eh?

**Joanne**   Sorry, no, it's just . . .

*Long pause.*

Sorry.

**Dave**   Yeah, well. Maybe it's not . . .

**Joanne**   You haven't changed.

**Dave**   Haven't I?

**Joanne**   Ten places at once. Have I come at a bad time?

**Dave**   Sorry?

**Joanne**   Shall I come back tomorrow?

*She begins removing her earrings and other jewellery.*

*Pause.*

I'm not 'ere t' fight with yer, Dave.

**Dave**   Sorry, I'm . . .

**Joanne**   Maybe I should just come back in the morning, eh?

**Dave**   No, I thought we'd take a walk.

**Joanne**   What?

**Dave**   I thought we'd take a walk down the South Bank tomorrow. By the river, I mean. The South Bank.

**Joanne**   My train leaves at ten.

**Dave**   Does it?

**Joanne**   Twenty past ten, Dave, yeah. Gets me back in just after lunch.

**Dave**   Oh, okay.

**Joanne**   I've got me IT class at three. What's down the South Bank?

**Dave**   No, nothing . . .

*Pause.*

Nothing, I just thought . . . −

**Joanne**   I mean I can always cancel.

**Dave**   It really doesn't matter.

**Joanne**   What's down there like?

*Pause.*

I'm interested, Dave . . . −

**Dave**   There's the market. Borough Market.

**Joanne**   Okay, fine.

**Dave**   The food there's fantastic.

**Joanne**   Is it?

**Dave**   Thought we could go on the Eye. The big wheel, yer must've seen it.

**Joanne**   I must've, yeah.

**Dave**   Amazing views.

**Joanne**   Yeah?

**Dave**   Yer can walk it from 'ere. Through the City.

**Joanne**   Great.

**Dave**   Stop by St Paul's. Over the Millennium Bridge. Tate Modern. Have a look down the Turbine Hall. Shakespeare's Globe.

**Joanne**   Whatever yer say, Dave.

**Dave**   Thought it might be nice, that's all. The two of us.

**Joanne**   'Ant you got work tomorrow?

**Dave**   What?

**Joanne**   Don't you work on a Friday?

**Dave**    Yeah, but . . . –

**Joanne**    Are yer sure they'll be alright with that?

**Dave**    That's not the point though is it?

**Joanne**    What is the point?

**Dave**    Nothin', I just thought . . .

*Pause.*

I just fuckin' thought.

**Joanne**    That's right, cos we don't go on walks back 'ome do we?

**Dave**    What?

**Joanne**    We're still livin' in caves, Dave, yeah.

**Dave**    They do a Jack the Ripper tour.

**Joanne**    They do what?

**Dave**    Up the road, up in Whitechapel. There's a Jack the Ripper tour.

*Pause.*

**Joanne**    I think I'll get that train if it's all the same.

**Dave**    I mean, there's Jamie Oliver's restaurant not five minutes . . . –

**Joanne**    Goodge Street.

**Dave**    What?

**Joanne**    My hotel. It's over in Goodge Street. That's the Central Line int it?

**Dave**    Northern.

**Joanne**    Is it?

**Dave**    Goodge Street's on the Northern Line.

**Joanne**    That's not what the man said.

**Dave**   Yer change at King's Cross.

**Joanne**   I'm glad I asked.

**Dave**   It's not far.

**Joanne**   Can't I walk it?

**Dave**   On the tube it's not far.

*Pause.*

Sorry. That sounded really patronising didn't it?

**Joanne**   Just a bit.

**Dave**   I'll order you a taxi if yer want.

**Joanne**   Yer'll do nothin' of the kind.

**Dave**   If yer'd prefer, I mean. In a bit.

**Joanne**   The tube's fine thanks.

**Dave**   I mean, if it's a question of money . . .

**Joanne**   It's not.

**Dave**   I don't mind, Joanne.

**Joanne**   It's not about the money, Dave, yer know that.

**Dave**   Sorry, yeah.

**Joanne**   I'm more than capable of takin' care of meself.

**Dave**   Yeah, I know . . . –

**Joanne**   You should know that by now.

**Dave**   I just said so didn't I?

**Joanne**   It's not like I 'ant 'ad the fuckin' practice.

**Dave**   *Question Time*'s on tonight.

**Joanne**   It's what?

**Dave**   *Question Time*. They've got Martin Amis on the panel, we could watch it.

*Long pause.*

*He makes to leave.*

Yeah, well, I'll just . . . –

**Joanne**    Yer think yer'll just what?

**Dave**    I think I'll 'ave somethin' stronger if yer don't mind.

**Joanne**    A drink?

**Dave**    A fuckin' bottle.

**Joanne**    You do that, Dave, yeah.

**Dave** *re-enters the living area, carrying* **Joanne**'s *shoes, tights, etc.*
*He dumps them on the futon, then moves to the kitchen area. He searches the cupboards and finds a bottle of brandy and a glass. He pours himself a shot and drinks it.*

*Pause.*

*He pours himself a triple shot and drinks another mouthful.*

*Pause.*

*He takes the brandy, moves to the office area and sits at his desk. Sipping the brandy, he ejects a CD from the laptop. With a marker pen, he writes something on the CD and places it in its case.*

*As he all does this,* **Joanne** *hesitates, then . . .*

*Pause.*

*She straightens the bed.*

*Pause.*

*She moves to the bedroom window and peers out at the buildings opposite.*

*She spies something or someone, and peers closer – her nose touching the glass.*

*Pause.*

*She returns to and sits on the edge of the bed.*
*She gets undressed.*

*She is about to remove her underwear, when . . .*
**Dave** *re-enters the bedroom, with his brandy and the CD.*

**Joanne**   D'yer know there's some Indian kid lookin' in?

**Dave**   Sorry?

**Joanne**   There's some Indian kid lookin' in from the flats out there.

*Pause.*

Dave . . . −

**Dave**   What, sorry?

**Joanne**   I mean he can't be much older than ten.

**Dave**   Oh, him.

**Joanne**   Peerin' through the curtains in his pyjamas, the dirty bastard.

**Dave**   Bangladeshi.

**Joanne**   What?

**Dave**   He's Bangladeshi, I think.

**Joanne**   Then he's a dirty Bangladeshi bastard.

**Dave**   Yeah, I know, he's always . . .

**Joanne** *removes her underwear.*

*Pause.*

**Joanne**   He's always what?

**Dave**   I think he must just be bored or somert.

**Joanne**   Yer've spoke to 'im?

**Dave**   I've seen 'im before, I mean.

**Joanne**   Yer should 'ave a word with 'is parents.

**Dave**   Well, I don't . . .

*Pause.*

Hardly breakin' the law though, is 'e?

**Joanne**    He wants to get 'imsen a girlfriend I reckon.

**Dave**    Yer don't want to encourage 'im, yer mean.

**Joanne**    'Ow d'yer know 'e's not goin' t' rob yer?

**Dave**    Eh?

**Joanne**    'Ow d'yer know 'e's not checkin' the place out?

**Dave**    He's not.

**Joanne**    'Ow d'yer know 'e's not workin' for a terrorist cell?

**Dave**    Yeah, alright . . .

**Joanne**    That's what they do down 'ere int it?

**Dave**    That's what who does exactly?

**Joanne**    Can't say I blame 'em neither. Your lot for neighbours.

**Dave**    Eh?

**Joanne**    Fuckin' iPod generation. I'd tell 'im to mind 'is bloody business if I were you.

*She reaches for her bag, and for her cigarettes.*
*She proceeds to light one.*

*Pause.*

**Dave** *places his brandy and the CD on the bedside cabinet.*
*He then moves to the blinds, and pulls them down.*

*Long pause.*

**Joanne**    Yer don't have to look so nervous, Dave.

**Dave**    Who said I was nervous?

**Joanne**    You out o' practice or somert?

**Dave**    No.

**Joanne**    Stood there like a bloody hatstand.

**Dave**    No, yer've had yer hair cut.

**Joanne**    What?

*Pause.*

**Dave**    I said yer've had yer hair cut, Joanne.

**Joanne**    Yeah, I have.

**Dave**    That recent?

**Joanne**    Fairly.

**Dave**    No, it suits yer.

**Joanne**    What?

**Dave**    I like it.

*Pause.*

Yer hair, I mean.

**Joanne**    D'yer?

**Dave**    It's nice.

*He sits on the edge of the bed.*

The colouring n' . . . n' that, it suits yer.

**Joanne**    Thanks.

*Long pause.*

**Dave** *goes to touch* **Joanne**'s hair.

**Dave**    I mean, yer'd never tell . . . –

**Joanne** (*pushes his hand away*)    Don't.

**Dave**    Sorry.

**Joanne**    Just don't alright?

**Dave**    Sorry, I dint . . . –

**Joanne**    Try that again and I'll fuckin' flatten yer.

**Dave**    No, I mean it, it's really . . .

*Long pause.*

It's really great to see you, Joanne.

**Joanne**    Don't tell me yer havin' second thoughts.

**Dave**    Of course not, it's just . . . –

**Joanne**    I'm ovulatin'.

**Dave**    What?

**Joanne**    I'm ovulatin'.

*Pause.*

**Dave**    Yeah, and that's a good thing isn't it?

**Joanne** *climbs into bed.*

*Long pause.*

**Dave**    Westminster Abbey.

**Joanne**    What?

**Dave**    The two of us, I mean.

**Joanne**    Yer thought the two of us might what?

**Dave**    I don't know, just . . .

*Pause.*

Anything.

**Joanne**    Yer thought we might go sightseein'?

**Dave**    No, not if yer don't want.

**Joanne**    Yer thought we might take a trip down memory lane?

**Dave**    Oh, come on, Joanne . . . –

**Joanne**    Like I'm supposed t' come fallin' into your arms or somert?

**Dave**    No, that's not it at all . . . –

**Joanne**    After all you put me through.

**Dave**    Don't be stupid.

**Joanne**    After ten years of fuckin' silence.

**Dave**    Don't be stupid, Joanne, no.

*Long pause.*

Of course not.

*Pause.*

I mean. Not if you don't . . . –

**Joanne**    There's some lad mags in me bag if yer need it.

**Dave**    Sorry?

**Joanne**    Only if yer need it mind.

*She picks up the copy of* Marie Claire, *and flicks through it.*

*Long pause.*

That is unless . . . –

**Dave**    No, I'm fine.

**Joanne**    They don't really go topless in *Marie Claire* d'they? Angelina Jolie, I mean. I don't suppose she'd ever . . . –

**Dave**    She doesn't, no, yer right.

**Joanne**    Pity.

**Dave**    Yeah.

**Joanne**    Most beautiful woman in the world.

**Dave**    T' some maybe.

**Joanne**    Big flappin' lips. CGI tits.

**Dave**    Monica Bellucci.

**Joanne**    Who?

**Dave**    Monica Bellucci, she's . . .

*Pause.*

Sorry.

**Joanne**    Who's Monica Bellucci when she's at 'ome?

**Dave**   No, just . . . –

**Joanne**   Whatever floats yer boat, Dave, come on.

**Dave**   It's not important.

**Joanne**   She a newsreader or somert?

**Dave**   A newsreader? No . . . –

**Joanne**   Kaplinsky.

**Dave**   It really doesn't matter.

**Joanne**   Natasha Kaplinsky.

**Dave**   What about 'er?

**Joanne**   I'd say she's right up your alley.

**Dave**   Yer takin' the piss.

**Joanne**   I'd say she's right up your beck n' call.

**Dave**   Yer takin' the piss, Joanne, give over.

**Joanne**   I know I'm takin' the piss.

**Dave**   No, I know, just . . .

*Over the following, the muffled – but audible – noise of drilling and hammering begins to be heard from the flat above.*

**Joanne** *pulls out a couple of lad mags from her handbag. She flicks through them.*

*Long pause.*

**Dave**   Joanne . . . –

**Joanne**   There's a feature on Abi Titmuss in this one.

**Dave**   What?

**Joanne**   Abi Titmuss, look.

*She flicks open the magazine for* **Dave** *and offers it to him.*

*Pause.*

**Joanne**   Aren't yer interested at least?

**Dave**    That's Abi Titmuss is it?

**Joanne**    She's got her tits out, Dave, yeah.

**Dave**    Oh.

*Long pause.*

Great, yeah . . . –

**Joanne**    Lucy Pinder. Sarah Harding.

**Dave**    Who?

**Joanne**    Girls Aloud. The blonde one.

**Dave**    Somethin' for everyone, yeah?

*Pause.*

Okay.

*He takes the other magazines.*

Okay, great . . . –

**Joanne**    I mean it's only if it helps.

**Dave**    It does help.

**Joanne**    Does it?

**Dave**    Yeah.

*Pause.*

Yeah, it's really helpful, Joanne.

**Joanne**    Course yer can always pay me back my train fare.

**Dave**    Yeah, I know.

**Joanne**    I mean if yer'd rather not . . . –

**Dave**    I've just said so 'ant I?

**Joanne**    I'd rather yer were honest with me, that's all.

**Dave**    I am being fuckin' honest.

**Joanne**    Yer know I'm goin' t' turn forty next month.

**Dave**    Yeah, I know that.

**Joanne**    Well then.

**Dave**    Jesus Christ, Joanne . . . –

**Joanne**    Yer fuckin' owe me this, you cunt.

*Long pause.*

**Dave**    Yeah, and I'm 'ere aren't I?

**Joanne**    Ten years of cleanin' up after your mess.

**Dave**    Alright, I know, it were me who wrote to you, remember?

**Joanne**    Oh, I remember alright.

**Dave**    Joanne, please . . . –

**Joanne**    I remember you flushin' our marriage down the toilet.

**Dave**    Alright, that's not what I meant.

**Joanne**    Betrayed and humiliated while you disappear to God knows where.

**Dave**    Oh, come off it, Joanne, . . .

**Joanne**    Beggin' for every penny I can lay my hands on, while you vanish into thin fuckin' air. Madeleine bleedin' McCann, yer lucky I don't charge by the hour.

**Dave**    That weren't it at all . . . –

**Joanne**    Weren't it?

**Dave**    You know that, Joanne.

**Joanne**    Forty year old wi' nowt but me fuckin' Freeview for company? I'd say that were pretty bang on.

**Dave**    I never abandoned anyone.

**Joanne**    Try tellin' that t' yer mother.

**Dave**    You leave her out o' this.

**Joanne**   We thought yer'd been killed f' fucksake!

*Long pause.*

**Dave**   I mean . . . –

**Joanne**   What's the tube of Canesten for?

**Dave**   Eh?

**Joanne**   'Ave you got thrush?

**Dave**   Don't be stupid.

**Joanne**   Chlamydia then?

**Dave**   No, I . . .

*Pause.*

I haven't, no.

**Joanne**   Good.

*Long pause.*

That's good then, Dave.

**Dave**   Yeah.

**Joanne**   I'm not goin' t' hang about forever.

**Dave**   No one's said that.

**Joanne**   We had an agreement dint we?

*Long pause.*

Dave . . . –

**Dave**   (*as he leaves*)   Just give me a minute would yer?

*He exits the bedroom, with the magazines, and enters the bathroom, slamming the door behind him.*
*He switches on the bathroom light.*
*He moves to the toilet, and places the magazines on the floor and the wine glass on the side of the bath.*

*While he does this,* **Joanne** *finishes her cigarette and stubs it out.*

*She makes to take the wine bottle, for which she has to climb out of bed to grab it from the chest of drawers, opposite the bed.*

*She takes the bottle of wine from off the chest of drawers.*

*Sitting on the edge of the bed, she takes her glass and refills it.*

*She then places the bottle back.*

*She sips from the wine glass.*

*Pause.*

*She catches sight of her reflection in the mirror.*

*Pause.*

*She pulls the covers up around her, disguising her body.*

*The drilling and hammering cause the lights in the flat to flicker momentarily.*

*Pause.*

*She looks back to her reflection, and messes with her hair.*

*She turns away from the mirror, and drinks from the wine glass.*

*The lights flicker momentarily.*

*Long pause.*

*She gathers the covers around her body, and climbs over the bed.*

*She moves to the full-length mirror and turns it round so that she can no longer see her reflection.*

*Pause.*

*She retrieves the bottle and the wine glass and refills it.*

*She drinks.*

*Long pause.*

*Pulling the covers around herself, she stands and heads to the window.*

*She peers through the blinds.*

*The lights flicker.*

*Long pause.*

*She opens the blinds a touch and looks through the window at the opposite flats.*

*As she does all this,* **Dave** *unbuckles his belt, and removes his trousers and pants.*

*He sits on the toilet seat.*

*He sips from his wine glass, then puts it back on the side of the bath.*

*He picks up the magazine and opens it up on the bookmarked page.*

*He plays with himself as he looks at the pictures.*

*The lights flicker.*

*Long pause.*

*He changes his mind, flicks through the magazine and finds another page.*

*He places the magazine on the floor, by his feet, folding the pages out, and using one of his feet as a paperweight.*

*Looking at the magazine, he takes another sip from his wine, and then proceeds to play with himself.*

*Long pause.*

*He grabs the towel that is hanging on the bathroom radiator.*

*He stands, then wraps and ties the towel around his waist.*

*He gathers his trousers and pants from the floor and holds them under one arm.*

*He exits the bathroom, and re-enters the bedroom.*
**Joanne** *is looking through the window, oblivious to his return.*

**Dave** *places his clothes by the side of the bed, then exits the bedroom.*

*He moves to and re-enters the bathroom.*

*He takes the magazine and the glass of wine.*

*He exits the bathroom, switching the light off as he goes.*

*He re-enters the bedroom, places the magazine on top of the letters on the bedside cabinet, and sits on the edge of the bed, holding his glass of wine.*

*The drilling and hammering continue, causing the lights to flicker.*

*Long pause.*

**Joanne** *pulls the blinds down and sits on the opposite end of the bed.*
*She finds another cigarette from the packet and lights it.*

*Long pause.*

**Joanne**　It's nice.

**Dave**　Sorry?

**Joanne**　The wine. It's very nice.

**Dave**　I think I'll stick t' the brandy if it's all the same.

**Joanne**　Got a fuckin' kick on it at least.

**Dave**　Yeah, thanks.

*Long pause.*

Yeah, it had a decent write-up.

**Joanne**　Did it?

**Dave**　Four stars.

**Joanne**　Oh . . .

**Dave**　In the . . . paper n' that. In the supplement.

**Joanne**　Oh, right.

*Long pause.*

**Dave**　And that's rare for Sainsbury's.

**Joanne**　I'll drink anything me.

**Dave**　I mean it's as good as owt yer'll find in Waitrose.

**Joanne**　Is it?

*Long pause.*

**Dave**　Yeah, it's . . . –

**Joanne**　Aren't yer goin' t' get in?

*Pause.*

Aren't yer goin' t' get it in with me, Dave?

*Long pause.*

D'yer need me to do anything for yer?

**Dave**   No, I'm . . .

*Pause.*

Really, I'm . . .

**Joanne**   Yer look like yer head's goin' to burst open.

**Dave**   Does it?

**Joanne**   Yer look like yer goin' t' combust, Dave, yeah. Does he always make that noise?

**Dave**   Yer'll get used to it.

**Joanne**   'Ow old is 'e? Twenty-eight?

**Dave**   Twenty-three.

**Joanne**   Shunt he be out livin' it up or somert?

**Dave**   Would yer like me to ask 'im for yer?

**Joanne**   He's hardly settin' the mood.

**Dave**   I'll ask 'im t' join us then shall I?

**Joanne**   I'm only sayin' . . . –

**Dave**   What d'yer want, the man from fuckin' Milk Tray?

**Joanne**   If it makes it any easier . . . –

**Dave**   How can it be any easier? Jesus Christ . . . –

**Joanne**   I'm jokin' with yer, yer dimwit.

**Dave**   D'yer see me fuckin' laughin'? Sat 'ere with me cock out.

**Joanne**   Oh, come on, Dave, it's not like we've never done it before.

**Dave**    Yeah, and I don't need you . . . −

**Joanne**    It's not like we're fuckin' strangers.

**Dave**    Yeah, I know that.

**Joanne**    We aborted three of 'em, remember?

*Long pause.*

**Dave**    Alright.

*Pause.*

Alright, just . . .

**Joanne**    I might need some warmin' up.

**Dave**    What?

**Joanne**    Yer might have t' warm me up.

*Long pause.*

Sorry.

**Dave**    No.

*Pause.*

No, that's . . .

**Joanne**    This isn't easy f'me either, yer know?

*Long pause.*

Please.

*Long pause.*

Dave . . . −

**Dave**    No, I know that.

**Joanne**    Wet yer fingers.

**Dave**    Eh?

**Joanne**    Wet yer fingers and yer thumb.

*She stubs her cigarette out.*

*Long pause.*

Well, go on.

*Pause.*

Go on, Dave.

**Dave**   I'm doin' it aren't I?

*He switches the bedside lamp off.*

*Darkness.*

*He removes the towel and climbs into bed with* **Joanne**, *pulling the covers over himself.*

*Long pause.*

*The sound of the hammering and drilling continues in short, muffled bursts.*

**Joanne**   Dave . . . −

**Dave**   Just a minute I said.

**Joanne**   But . . . −

**Dave**   Give me a minute.

*Long pause.*

**Joanne**   Can't yer find it?

*Long pause.*

Can't yer find it?

*Pause.*

Just . . . there.

*Pause.*

Just there. That's it, right there.

*Pause.*

Where yer were before.

*Pause.*

Where yer were, go on. It's not a punchbag.

*Very, very long pause.*

Don't do that, Dave −

**Dave** *climbs out from under the sheets.*

**Joanne**   Dave, please . . . −

**Dave**   I can't think straight.

**Joanne**   You just had it, go on.

**Dave**   I can't fuckin' think straight, Joanne.

*He switches the bedside lamp on.*

*He climbs off **Joanne**, and sits on the edge of the bed.*

*He pulls the towel back over his waist and legs.*

*Long pause.*

**Joanne** *takes her drink from the bedside cabinet and sips it.*

**Dave** *doesn't move from the edge of the bed.*

*Long pause.*

**Joanne**   Here.

**Dave**   What?

**Joanne**   Here.

*She hands **Dave** her drink.*

**Joanne**   Quiet as mice, go on.

**Joanne** *kneels up on the bed, behind **Dave** and strokes his shoulders and chest.*

*Long pause.*

**Joanne**   That okay f'yer?

*Long pause.*

**Joanne** *strokes* **Dave***'s body, then slips her hand under the towel.*

*Long pause.*

**Joanne**    Dave.

*She has her hand under the towel, between* **Dave***'s legs.*

*Long pause.*

**Joanne**    Tell me if I'm . . . –

*Pause.*

Tell me if I'm pullin' it too 'ard.

*Pause.*

If yer want me t' pull the skin back.

*Pause.*

If yer want me squeeze the tip.

**Dave**    The wireless is switched on.

*Long pause.*

**Joanne**    Dave.

*Long pause.*

Is there somethin' the . . . ?

**Dave**    The fuckin' wireless is switched on.

*He pulls* **Joanne***'s hand out from under the towel.*

**Joanne**    But . . . –

**Dave**    The wireless, Joanne, just stop it will yer?!

*Pause.*

**Joanne**    Are you alright?

**Dave**    I've left it hooked up t' the computer –

**Joanne**    Yer've left what?

**Dave**    Don't you laugh at me.

**Joanne**    I'm not laughing.

**Dave**    Don't you dare laugh at me, Joanne, I mean it!

*He slams the wine glass on the cabinet, then grabs his clothes off the floor and, over the following, frantically gets dressed.*

*Pause.*

Laugh in my fuckin' face. D'yer know what that's meant t' do t' yer?!

**Joanne**    Alright, I won't.

**Dave**    D'yer know what that does t' yer brain cells, Joanne?! F' Christ's sake . . . −

*He exits the bedroom, carrying the rest of his clothes, and enters the living space.*
*The noise of the drilling is getting louder.*
*He moves to the futon, sits.*

*(As he sits.)*    − . . . you've only just walked in through the fuckin' door!

*He pulls on and buttons up the rest of his clothes.*

Stupid fuckin' . . . −

*Following this,* **Dave** *moves to the office area, and wrestles with the cables in an attempt to unplug the wireless and shut down his computer.*

*Through all this,* **Joanne** *wraps the sheets around herself, and exits the bedroom.*
*She stands by the bedroom doorway, watching* **Dave**.

**Joanne**    Is there somethin' yer want t' talk about?

**Dave** *continues.*

*Pause.*

**Joanne**    Dave . . . −

**Dave**    I'm doin' it aren't I?

**Joanne**    I mean, it's nothin' . . . −

**Dave**   Just leave it, Joanne!

**Joanne**   It's nothin' to be ashamed of . . . −

**Dave**   I can't think!

**Joanne**   Alright . . . −

**Dave**   I can't think with all 'is fuckin' noise! Gi' over fuckin' followin' me will yer?!

*He throws the cables back down, and makes for the front door.*

*Pause.*

**Joanne**   Dave . . . −

**Dave** (*as he exits*)   This is my fuckin' flat, stay where you are!

*He exits through the front door, slamming the door behind him.*

*The drilling and hammering continues.*

*Long pause.*

**Joanne** *re-enters the bedroom, and sits on the edge of the bed.*

*She takes her glass of wine and sips from it.*

*Pause.*

*She puts the wine glass down.*

*She picks up her underwear and puts it back on.*

*Pause.*

*She goes to pick up the rest of her clothes from the floor, when . . .*

*Pause.*

*She spots the tracksuit bottoms and T-shirt that **Dave** hid under the bed.*

*She pulls them out.*

*She looks at them. The T-shirt has a printed logo on the front: 'The Libertines' or 'Arctic Monkeys', or a similar rock band.*

*Pause.*

*She puts the T-shirt and the tracksuit bottoms on.*

*The drilling and hammering upstairs suddenly stops.*

*Long pause.*

*She moves before the mirror.*

*She looks at her reflection, dressed in the new outfit.*

*Pause.*

*She strikes a pose.*

*Pause.*

*She messes up her hair.*

*She strikes a pose.*

*Pause.*

*She returns to the edge of the bed and sits down.*

*She takes a cigarette from her packet, puts it in her mouth (in the style of Keith Richards), and lights it.*

*Pause.*

*She hesitates.*

*Pause.*

*She moves to the bedroom window.*

*She pulls the blinds up, and peers out to the opposite flats.*

*Pause.*

*She taps on the window with her knuckles.*

*Pause.*

*Standing before the window she takes off the 'Libertines' T-shirt.*

*Pause.*

*She removes her bra.*

*Pause.*

*She peers out of the window.*

*Pause.*

*She taps on the window with her knuckles, when . . .*

**Dave** *re-enters through the front door, shutting the door behind him.*

*He stands by the doorway and buttons up his shirt.*

**Joanne** *pulls the blinds down.*

*Pause.*

**Joanne** *returns to the edge of the bed, and stubs out her cigarette.*

*She puts on the T-shirt.*

*As she does this, and over the next,* **Dave** *straightens his shirt and moves to the office area.*

*He sits at his desk.*

*He removes his mobile phone from his pocket, turns it on, and checks/ scrolls through a couple of new text messages.*

*The following dialogue takes place between the two rooms.*

**Joanne** (*from the bedroom*)    Feelin' better now are yer?

*Long pause.*

Dave.

**Dave** (*from the living area*)    What, sorry?

**Joanne** (*from the bedroom*)    Everythin' alright?

**Dave** (*from the living area*)    I think we'll be alright for a bit, yeah.

*Pause.*

Before the evening's out at least.

**Joanne** (*from the bedroom*)    Punch his lights out did yer?

**Dave** (*from the living area*)    No, it's his bathroom.

**Joanne** (*from the bedroom*)    It's his what?

**Dave** (*from the living area*)    He's doin' up his bathroom.

**Joanne** (*from the bedroom*)   Oh, right.

**Dave** (*from the living area*)   Yeah.

*Pause.*

Yeah, it's lookin' pretty good. Mirrors on both walls.

**Joanne** (*from the bedroom*)   That's good then int it?

**Dave** (*from the living area*)   Power shower. Remote sensor . . .

*Pause.*

Remote sensor thingamajig.

**Joanne** (*from the bedroom*)   Don't tell me yer jealous.

**Dave** (*from the living area*)   Fuck off, jealous. What, of him?

**Joanne** (*from the bedroom*)   I'm only sayin'.

**Dave** (*from the living area*)   That little nondescript? – Yeah, well don't.

**Joanne** (*from the bedroom*)   If you're going to get stroppy about it . . . –

**Dave** (*from the living area*)   Arrogant bastard.

**Joanne** (*from the bedroom*)   What did you call me?

**Dave** (*from the living area*)   I said he's an arrogant little bastard.

*Long pause.*

**Dave** *finishes reading his text messages and tosses the mobile phone on the desk.*

*He hesitates, while . . .*

**Joanne** *sparks another cigarette, placing the pack in the tracksuit-bottom pocket.*

*She stands and picks up the two wine glasses.*

**Dave** *moves to, and enters, the bathroom, shutting the door behind him.*

**Joanne** *exits the bedroom, and enters the living area.*

*She goes to the kitchen area, and places the wine glasses on the counter.*

*She finds the wine bottle.*

*She proceeds to pour two fresh glasses of wine.*

*As she does this,* **Dave** *moves to the toilet, and lifts up the lid.*

*He has a piss.*

*Pause.*

*He accidentally pisses on the floor.*

*Pause.*

*He flushes the toilet, and grabs a length of toilet roll.*

*He squats down on the floor, and wipes the piss up off the floor and from around the basin/rim.*

*He throws the toilet paper into the toilet.*

*Pause.*

*He moves to the sink, and washes his hands.*

*While he does this,* **Joanne** *has filled up the wine glasses.*

*She rummages through the cupboards, and removes the ingredients for the chorizo and cannellini-bean salad.*

*She places these on the side.*

*Meanwhile,* **Dave** *turns off the taps and is about to exit the bathroom.*

*Pause.*

*He hesitates.*

*Pause.*

*He returns to the toilet, shuts the lid and sits down.*

*Pause.*

*He hesitates.*

*Pause.*

*He rummages through his pockets.*

*As he does this, the mobile phone that he abandoned on the desk begins to vibrate.*

**Joanne** *sees/hears the phone vibrating.*

*She hesitates.*

*Pause.*

*She leaves the kitchen area, and moves to the desk.*

*She is about to pick up the phone, but it stops ringing.*

*Pause.*

**Dave** *stops rummaging through his pockets.*

*Pause.*

*He hesitates, while . . .*

**Joanne** *picks up the phone and returns to the kitchen area, placing it on the counter.*

*She unwraps the chorizo sausage from its packaging, while . . .*

**Dave** *stands and, quickly checking his reflection in the mirror, exits the bathroom, shutting the door behind him.*

*He moves through the living space, and enters the bedroom.*

*Pause.*

*He sits on the bed, and looks for his socks and shoes.*

*He finds them and puts them on.*

*As he does this,* **Joanne** *finds a knife and begins to chop the chorizo sausage.*

*Pause.*

*The mobile phone vibrates.*

**Joanne** *picks up the phone, presses a button and puts it to her ear.*

*Long pause.*

**Dave** *has put on his socks and shoes.*

*He stands and goes to the bedside cabinet.*

*He picks up the CD.*
*He opens the lid, closes the lid.*

*Pause.*

*He looks for his glass of wine, but cannot find it.*

*As* **Joanne** *finishes listening to the voice message and presses a button to end the call . . .*

**Dave** *re-enters the living space, with the CD.*

*He hesitates.*

**Joanne** *puts the phone back on the kitchen counter.*

*She hesitates.*

*Long pause.*

**Dave** *moves to the kitchen area, and takes his glass of wine.*

*Pause.*

*He moves to the office area and sits by the desk.*

*He places the CD on the desk, and sips his wine.*

*Pause.*

**Joanne** *takes the kitchen knife and begins chopping up the chorizo sausage.*

**Dave** *peers through the blinds.*

*Pause.*

*He watches* **Joanne**.

*Pause.*

*He picks up the CD.*

*Long pause.*

**Dave**   I burnt yer a CD.

**Joanne**   Did yer?

**Dave**   Yeah, I . . .

*Pause.*

Burnt yer a few tunes yer might like.

**Joanne**   Oh . . . –

**Dave**   Somethin' t' take back with yer, I mean. Somethin' f' when yer get home.

**Joanne**   Oh, that's nice.

**Dave**   Yeah, I mean that's . . .

*Pause.*

That's what I thought.

**Joanne**   Has it got any Beatles on it?

**Dave**   One or two.

**Joanne**   I am surprised.

**Dave**   No, I was thinkin' of you, I mean.

**Joanne**   I see.

**Dave**   There's a track-listin' on the box. I think yer'll like it.

**Joanne**   No, I'm sure . . . –

**Dave**   Just, yer know?

**Joanne**   Thanks, that's . . .

**Dave**   Some songs yer might not 'ave got.

*Long pause.*

'She Bangs the Drums'.

**Joanne**   Who?

**Dave**   'She Bangs the Drums'.

**Joanne**   Oh . . .

**Dave**   The Stone Roses.

**Joanne**   Oh, yeah, that's . . .

**Dave** 'Waterfall' n' that. Yer know?

*Pause.*

Couple off *The Second Coming*.

*Pause.*

'Ten Storey Love Song'. Some of the mellower . . . –

**Joanne** That's very kind of yer, Dave, yeah.

**Dave** Takes yer back though dunt it? Me n' you like. '89.

*Long pause.*

I mean, I can stick it on now if yer'd rather.

*Long pause.*

I can play it through the plasma screen, through the speakers. Yer'd be astonished at the quality.

*Long pause.*

I can stick the fuckin' thing on now, Joanne.

**Joanne** *snatches the CD off* **Dave**.
*She inspects the track list.*

*Pause.*

This your idea of foreplay?

**Dave** No.

**Joanne** Well I should hope not n' all.

**Joanne** *reads the track-listing on the CD.*

*Pause.*

**Dave** No. I just thought . . . –

**Joanne** Elvis Costello, Sam Cooke.

**Dave** Yeah.

*Pause.*

Yeah, it's . . . –

**Joanne**　Not many women on this is there?

**Dave**　There's Joni Mitchell.

**Joanne** *puts the CD down and continues chopping the chorizo.*

*Long pause.*

**Dave**　I made it for you, Joanne.

*Long pause.*

Joanne . . . –

**Joanne**　Yeah, I heard yer the first time.

**Dave**　It belongs to me.

**Joanne**　Alright . . . –

**Dave**　No, the plasma screen, it's mine.

*Pause.*

That and the laptop, the whole . . .

*Pause.*

. . . the whole set-up, I mean. The wardrobe through there, the blinds. The fuckin' pictures on the walls.

**Joanne**　They're all yours are they?

**Dave**　The crockery, Joanne, yeah. – Don't think I 'ant got plans.

**Joanne**　I don't.

**Dave**　Don't think I can't see the bigger picture.

**Joanne**　Did I say that?

**Dave**　Yer don't 'ave t' say a thing, Joanne, no, I'll take yer shoppin' if yer want.

**Joanne**　What?

**Dave**　I'll take yer down Knightsbridge. Harrods, I mean.

*Pause.*

Yeah, I will.

*Pause.*

I'll treat yer, Joanne, yer'd like that.

*Long pause.*

Yer'd like that, Joanne, I know yer would.

**Joanne**    I'd like yer to gi' over fuckin' whinin'.

**Dave**    Yer used t' bloody live for it, come on.

**Joanne**    Falsetto fuckin' whinin' in my ear, yer as bad as each other.

**Dave**    D'yer know how hard I work at my job?

**Joanne**    No, you tell me.

**Dave**    Have you any idea of the hours I put in?

**Joanne**    Tell me all about it, Dave, go on.

**Dave**    I could buy you a fuckin' diamond with what I earn. – This big, Joanne, don't look at me like that, I'll do it n' all.

**Joanne**    Can I have that in writin'?

**Dave**    Name the price.

**Joanne**    What?

**Dave**    Name the price.

**Joanne**    I'd settle f' some semen, thanks. – What? Are yer not man enough f' that?

*Long pause.*

**Dave**    Alright, Joanne, don't . . . –

**Joanne**    Don't what? Don't belittle yer? I think yer've done a good enough job o' that already don't you?

**Dave**    Look, I shunt have to explain t' you again . . .

**Joanne**    Shoutin' yer mouth off.

**Dave**    Eh?

**Joanne**    Shoutin' yer mouth off at me. What, are yer Captain fuckin' Caveman or somert?

**Dave**    I told yer, I can't . . . –

**Joanne**    Captain Caveman, raise yer fist at me.

*She chops the chorizo.*

*Long pause.*

Should've just said if yer weren't up to it.

**Dave**    I am up to it.

**Joanne**    Waste my time.

**Dave**    I'm fuckin' up to it, Joanne, alright?

**Joanne**    Go back on yer promise.

**Dave**    I told yer I can't think with that noise.

**Joanne**    Impotent old bastard.

*Long pause.*

What, did it just slip yer mind to fuckin' tell me?

**Dave**    It's a studio flat.

**Joanne**    It's what?

**Dave**    It's a studio flat, for Christ's sake, yer get what you pay for. I can't stop other people . . .

**Joanne** *continues chopping the chorizo.*

*Long pause.*

**Dave**    Sleep on 'ere.

**Joanne**    What?

**Dave**    No, I mean, I can. I can do that, I mean.

*Pause.*

I can sleep on the futon tonight, I don't mind.

**Joanne**  Oh . . . –

**Dave**  No, I'd like that.

**Joanne**  Would yer?

**Dave**  I'd be more than happy, Joanne.

**Joanne**  Right.

**Dave**  Yer've always hated hotels anyway.

**Joanne** *chops the chorizo.*

*Long pause.*

**Dave**  Remember?

*Long pause.*

Remember, Joanne?

*Long pause.*

Jesus Christ, put it down will yer?

*She continues.*

*Long pause.*

I don't want yer doin' that.

**Joanne**  Yer look like yer goin' t' pass out.

**Dave**  Put it down I said.

**Joanne**  Yer look like yer could do wi' it, Dave, yer've gone pale.

**Dave**  Put the knife down, will yer?

*Pause.*

Yer not even using it right.

**Joanne**  Yeah, well, you were the one . . . –

**Dave**  D'yer know how much that cost me?

**Joanne**  You're the one insistin' we stuff our fuckin' faces.

**Dave**  That's Sabatier, yer dimwit!

*She continues.*

*Long pause.*

I'm warnin' you, Joanne.

*Pause.*

I'm more than capable of cooking my own fuckin' supper.

*Long pause.*

Look, give it over, come on.

**Joanne**  Don't you touch me.

**Dave**  The fuckin' knife, I said, yer going to wreck it.

*Long pause.*

The fucking knife . . . −

*He wrestles the knife out of her hand, and pushes her aside.*

. . . Joanne, hand it over!

**Joanne**  Ow! Don't you fuckin' . . . −

**Dave**  Give it back to me, sit down!

**Joanne**  Grab at me, Dave, I'll . . . −

**Dave**  Sit down! . . . −

*Over the next, **Dave** grabs **Joanne** and drags her out of the kitchen area and into the living space, throwing her down onto the futon.*

**Dave**  Sit the fuck down, get down!

**Joanne**  (*fighting back*)  Yer mad fuckin' bastard . . . −

**Dave**  (*dragging her*)  Get away from me, you 'ear?

**Joanne**  (*fighting back*)  Don't you ever touch me like . . . −

**Dave** *shoves* **Joanne** *onto the futon.*

**Dave**   Sit down and shut up!

**Joanne**   Grab at me, yer fuckin' maniac!

**Dave**   Yeah, and yer can take that fuckin' T-shirt off n' all.

**Joanne**   I can take what off? Don't you come near me –

**Dave**   Take it off, it's not yours!

**Joanne**   Don't touch me, don't . . . –

**Dave**   Take it off I said . . . –

*He grabs* **Joanne** *and tries pulling the tracksuit bottoms and top off her.* **Joanne** *fights back, punching, kicking and scratching him.*

**Dave**   . . . Take it off! I'll rip yer fuckin' head off, Joanne, come on!

**Joanne**   Jesus Christ . . . –

**Dave**   It dunt fuckin' belong to you!

**Joanne**   Hands off me, hands . . . –

*She boots and scratches* **Dave** *away.*

**Joanne**   . . . off!

**Dave**   It dunt belong to you, they're not yours!

**Joanne**   You try that one more fuckin' time.

**Dave**   Yer'll do as I fuckin' well . . . –

*He grabs the knife from the side.*

. . . tell yer, Joanne, you 'ear?!

*Long pause.*

Joanne . . . –

**Joanne**   D'yer want me to call the police?

**Dave**   It's gone, look, it's gone.

*He puts the knife down on the counter.*

*Long pause.*

I've put it down, Joanne, see?

*Long pause.*

Joanne.

*He slowly moves towards her.*

*Long pause.*

Joanne, please . . . –

**Joanne**   Yer bleedin', look.

**Dave**   What?

**Joanne**   There's blood runnin' down your face.

**Dave** *touches his face.*
*There are scratch marks on his forehead and cheeks that are bleeding. He sees the blood on his fingers.*

*Long pause.*

**Dave**   Oh . . .

*Pause.*

Oh. Yeah, that's . . .

**Joanne**   That's blood, Dave, yeah. Will she be alright with that?

**Dave**   Will who be alright? – I've told yer before, she's nothin'.

**Joanne**   How are yer goin' to explain that one at work?

*Pause.*

Dave . . . –

**Dave**   I'm not.

**Joanne**   Won't they be bothered?

**Dave**   No, I'm not . . . –

**Joanne**   All the hours yer put in.

**Dave**   Look . . . –

**Joanne**   The amount you earn.

**Dave**   I'm not going to do that, Joanne, fuck off will yer?

**Joanne**   They won't be bothered then I take it. – Are they not bothered about you?

**Dave**   Look . . . –

**Joanne**   Are you that much of a nondescript?

**Dave**   I don't have to explain myself to anyone.

**Joanne**   Does anyone even notice that you're there? What d'yer do again?

**Dave**   I'm not goin' t' let you . . . –

**Joanne**   What's yer job title again?

**Dave**   Eh?

**Joanne**   What d'they call yer? – It's not a trick question, Dave.

**Dave**   I've told yer before, it's an agency.

**Joanne**   It's what?

**Dave**   I work for an agency.

**Joanne**   What agency?

**Dave**   A recruitment agency, I'm freelance. – Jesus Christ, what is this?

**Joanne**   Alright, I'm only askin'.

**Dave**   What are yer, the Inland Revenue now?

**Joanne**   I'm only tryin' t' paint a picture . . . –

**Dave**   Shall I print you off a CV while yer at it?

**Joanne**   No . . . –

**Dave**    Fuckin' remittance.

**Joanne**    What?

**Dave**    My fuckin' remittance, look! 'Ere!

*He grabs a letter from the desk, and throws it at* **Joanne**.

**Dave**    Bloody Bergerac yer! I swear to God . . . –

**Joanne**    Yer gettin' hysterical again, Dave.

**Dave**    Get it fuckin' framed, go on!

**Joanne**    I think yer'd better . . . –

**Dave**    Hang it t' the bedroom ceilin' why not!

**Joanne**    I think yer should calm down don't you?

**Dave**    I am fuckin' calm!

*He moves to the kitchen area and refills his wine glass.*

Jesus Christ, Joanne, have you totally lost the fuckin' plot?

**Joanne**    Beatin' up on women.

**Dave**    I did what?

**Joanne**    Pushin' me around.

**Dave**    Oh, come on, grow up.

**Joanne**    Is this how you get your kicks or somert?

**Dave**    I hardly touched yer f' fucksake. I hardly touched yer, don't . . . –

**Joanne**    Does she know about your problem?

**Dave**    What problem? If you think . . . –

**Joanne**    You n' yer limp fuckin' dick.

**Dave**    Joanne, please . . . –

**Joanne**    Well, does she?

*Pause.*

**Dave**  Look . . . –

**Joanne**  Does she sit n' nod n' blame herself for your hang-ups? That pitiful fuckin' stump?

**Dave**  That's not . . .

**Joanne**  I bet yer bloody let 'er n' all, poor bitch.

**Dave**  Yer know nothin' about 'er, Joanne, it's different.

**Joanne**  What?

**Dave**  It's just different, alright? For Christ's sake . . . –

**Joanne**  Off 'er face on God knows what.

**Dave**  It's different when it's someone who knows what they're doin' at least.

**Joanne**  Excuse me?

**Dave**  That's right, Joanne, yeah. When it's not some overweight, middle-aged cunt, dressed up like a schoolteacher. When it's a bleached-blonde nineteen-year-old with tits like two meringues. When we've been up all night snortin' charlie and she's suckin' off the end o' my cock. – Yeah, that makes a difference, Joanne, is that alright f'yer is it? Bloody milk monitor, look. It's different when 'er cunt's still got some leverage in it n' all. It's different when there's somert left t' fuckin' feel up there. When it's not some splayed-out old gammon yer'd need a bloody wheelie bin just t' work up the tiniest bit o' friction.

**Joanne**  It's different is it?

**Dave**  It's different, Joanne, don't get me started.

**Joanne**  'Ave yer told 'er we're still married?

**Dave**  No.

**Joanne**  Are you plannin' to?

**Dave**  No.

*Pause.*

No, I'm . . . –

**Joanne**    She doesn't know then I take it?

**Dave**    Look . . . –

**Joanne**    She doesn't know about the debts you left me and my family with?

**Dave**    That's not the . . . –

**Joanne**    The thousands o' pounds I'm still payin' off.

**Dave**    That's not the fuckin' point, Joanne!

*Pause.*

No, of course not, I've told yer, it's . . . –

**Joanne**    It's nothin', yeah, I gathered that.

**Dave**    She's insignificant, Joanne, I hardly know her.

**Joanne**    'Ow come she's screaming down the phone at yer then?

**Dave**    She's what?

**Joanne**    Have you had a fallin'-out or somert?

**Dave**    She said what, sorry?

**Joanne**    They're on their way to the Academy.

**Dave**    Where?

**Joanne**    Brixton Academy. Some Grime Night apparently.

**Dave**    Some what night?

**Joanne**    That's right, Dave, they're about to get the tube if yer hurry up. Her and this Denzil bloke whoever he is. Somert about needin' to pay the man off like yer promised.

**Dave**    Look . . . –

**Joanne**    Are you supplyin' 'er with drugs, Dave?

**Dave**    Don't be stupid.

**Joanne**    D'yer want me to call 'er back?

**Dave**   Joanne, please . . . –

**Joanne**   I think yer should do that, Dave, actually. I mean, Christ knows . . . –

**Dave**   She can take care of herself.

**Joanne**   She can what?

**Dave**   She's more than capable, Joanne.

**Joanne**   Oh, I'm sure she's capable alright.

**Dave**   No, they're to help her lose weight. The drugs, I mean, the money.

**Joanne**   They're doing what?

**Dave**   She's trying to get into the fashion industry, I don't know.

**Joanne**   No, yer don't know.

**Dave**   It's a lifestyle, it costs money.

**Joanne**   What, and you're her manager are yer?

**Dave**   I hardly know her f' fucksake.

**Joanne**   Are you her pimp, Dave?

**Dave**   We met at a nightclub, it was her who came on to me!

**Joanne**   Yeah, I bet she did.

**Dave**   Oh, come on, Joanne . . . –

**Joanne**   Yeah, I bet she saw you comin'. You n' yer plasma screen.

**Dave**   Are you jealous or somethin'?

**Joanne**   You n' yer diamond bloody rings, givin' it the great big lovable bear. Some teenager who dunt know any better . . . –

**Dave**   She's goin' t' turn twenty in October, of course she dunt know any better, she can work that out for herself!

**Joanne**   Some girl you leave to wander the streets like that.

**Dave**   Look, if I thought for one minute that she was even remotely . . . –

**Joanne**   What, yer'd be chargin' out that door?

**Dave**   Let me finish.

**Joanne**   Yer'd be racin' over to Brixton in yer Batmobile would yer?

**Dave**   Yer'd know about it.

**Joanne**   What?

**Dave**   Yer'd fuckin' know about it, Joanne.

**Joanne**   Oh, come off it, yer donkey, yer've only ever been bothered about yerself. They could be wheelin' 'er down A&E for all you fuckin' care. Like you care about any one of us.

**Dave**   That's not true.

**Joanne**   You n' yer flash fuckin' flat.

**Dave**   Alright . . . –

**Joanne**   You n' yer Gucci fuckin' suit.

**Dave**   Alright, just . . .

**Joanne**   Actin' the big man.

**Dave**   Just settle down . . . –

**Joanne**   Don't act the big man with me, yer fat fuckin' bastard, I can still see straight through yer.

**Dave**   But I wasn't . . . –

**Joanne**   Fuckin' caretaker you.

**Dave**   I wasn't trying to do anything, Joanne –

**Joanne**   Yer tenant.

**Dave**   What?

**Joanne**   You temporary tenant. – 'Ow old are yer now?

**Dave**  I'm forty-fuckin'-four.

**Joanne**  Walled up in this shit'ole.

**Dave**  This is a prime location for Christ's sake!

**Joanne**  I know what I see.

**Dave**  We're in the centre of London, Joanne, look around yer!

**Joanne**  I know a shit'ole when I see one.

**Dave**  When you see one!

**Joanne**  That's right, Dave, yeah, I'm not one of yer little air'eads, I can see with my own two eyes . . . –

**Dave**  Oh, face it, Joanne, you 'ant got the class.

**Joanne**  I 'ant got the what?

**Dave**  You 'ant got the class, yer block'ead. – What did you expect? The Houses of bloody Parliament?

**Joanne**  Don't you talk down to me like that.

**Dave**  Get yer facts straight then, retard, this is the centre of London, we're only five minutes from the Bank of England out there.

**Joanne**  At least I still know where I come from.

**Dave**  Oh, fuck off, 'come from'. Yer'll be pullin' out yer flat cap next!

**Joanne**  Yer don't even know who you are any more.

**Dave**  And I suppose yer'd rather it were somert off Brookside bloody Close would yer?

**Joanne**  At least I don't . . . –

**Dave**  Some leafy fuckin' cul-de-sac with its own piss-stained fuckin' Spar. Some two-up two-down with a plastic fuckin' playground out the back. Scrappin' over a bag o' soggy chips with the rest of the provincial primates. That's what you all aspire to int it? Some wet God-awful nightmare of the Northern working class, yeah, I'm green with fuckin' envy I am, Joanne, yer've put yer finger on the button there, well done.

**Joanne**   So that's why you abandoned us is it?

**Dave**   We were dead already, Joanne, let's not get petty.

**Joanne**   What, were it not minimalist enough for yer?

**Dave**   The space between your ears, woman, yer know what I'm fuckin' talkin' about.

**Joanne**   Abandoned it, that house! After all we'd been workin' towards . . . –

**Dave**   We were finished, yer fuckin' idiot, I didn't have that choice!

**Joanne**   That's right, Dave, I remember.

**Dave**   'Abandon you'! Jesus Christ, I was suffocating up there!

**Joanne**   Come back home t' some note left on the mantelpiece. Some eight-year-old scrawl tellin' me t' move back in with me dad, yeah, that's really fuckin' petty.

**Dave**   It were over between us anyway, yer know that!

**Joanne**   Ten years I've been waitin' on you, David Harrison.

**Dave**   Yeah, and it's taken me ten years just to even try and rectify some of the damage . . . –

**Joanne**   F' me to absolve you, yer mean.

**Dave**   F' me to look you in the face. F' me to try and make sense of all the effort I made . . . –

**Joanne**   The effort you made?

**Dave**   All the effort it took me to just get out the bed of a morning. The effort to be able to look my wife in the face and not feel like I'm going to batter the shit out of her. – Are yer listening?

**Joanne**   Yeah.

**Dave**    Because I look into the future and all I see is shit. I take every possible outcome given who I am and what I do, and all the fucking maybes and small talk on that piece of shit bastard sofa – the one you forced me to buy on our account I might add, another fuckin' five years' worth of interest. Interest we'd still be payin' off t' this day, Joanne, don't pretend yer don't know. – You know, it's written all over yer, it was just like everythin' else. The sofa, the car, the house, the fuckin' never-endin' wardrobe upstairs. Working my arse off t' support some life that I were never even fit for, that were rotten with the stink o' dead babies. The babies we aborted. The babies we postponed, Joanne. The ones dependent on my solvency, the ones I had you murder. – Oh, don't worry, I 'ant forgot. How the fuck could I? I've been strugglin' t' face up t' that promise since I first caught the train straight out o' that moronic arsehole of a town. The years n' months together, those three little bastards and their mother I doubt I ever loved. This woman who wanted the world and everything in it, but who could never stand accountable because she couldn't decide what the fuck she was supposed to be anyway. Jesus Christ, I should've left you in a shot had I had more sense, had I not listened to you and owned up to my own financial inadequacy. Oh, that is what you called it eventually though int it? The inadequate, the bankrupt? – Had we not been so dependent on the little income that we actually had that the very idea of separation meant death. Stuck in that house for five years, while I'm staring into this never-ending vacuum and deludin' myself like every other wanker out there, that what? That democracy makes me special? That because I'm not born in some East African fuckin' village somewhere, that I'm somehow entitled to my success? That with hard work and perseverance alone I could be one of a thousand other people than the fat lonely bastard that I really am. Because, yer know what, Joanne? When I met you, all I wanted t' do was t' be in a fuckin' rock band. A rock band, Joanne, you didn't even enter into it. If I could play the guitar like John Squire, if I could bash a fuckin' chord out at least, if I could live – I mean, how pathetic is that? If I could live in some faraway fucking fantasy land and that that alone might take me away, take me out of this skin,

take away everythin' I grew up with, Joanne. The fuckin'
shadow of Margaret Thatcher, watchin' her drain the last
ounce o' hope out o' my own father. – If I could just sell one
of me third-rate fuckin' stories at least, Jesus Christ, what was
I thinkin'? What were you thinkin' more to the point? Wavin'
around some English degree that never got me anywhere. Job
after miserable job, dependent on some miracle, some mythical
promotion that never fuckin' happened, that were never going
to happen, that I 'ant got the talent for, Joanne, let's face it.
The weeks and months just slippin' through my fingers, while
you, in your Buddha-like compassion, continue to spend and
you spend and you spend and you spend. The handbags and
the shoes. Booking fucking holidays behind my back while
I'm cracking my brain open just t' make up the minimum
payments, and for what? For a life that was always going to
be beyond us. For a life that was always going to pass us by. For
a life built on credit cards and debit schemes, this towering
fuckin' inventory of plastic, of borrowed goods and lowered
interest rates, and consolidated fuckin' repayment plans that they
threw at us like sweets, the bastards. The dirty, unaccountable
bastards. The voice on the end of the phone who offers yer the
world if yer only prepared to pay for it later. And that I could
never repay! And that I built n' furnished your house with,
Joanne, and who I killed your children with, and that you, like
a dunce, placed into my trust. – And what? Yer think that
didn't take some effort? You think you were the only one? You
think that all the promises you bullied me into . . . ?

**Joanne**    The promises you broke, yer mean.

**Dave**    That I can't even cut it as a human fuckin' being.
D'yer want t' know how that feels?

*Long pause.*

I was thinkin' of hangin' myself.

**Joanne**    Were yer?

**Dave**    I was thinkin' of doin' that, Joanne, yeah.

**Joanne**    Oh.

**Dave**   I thought I'd explained all that in my letters.

*Pause.*

**Joanne**   Oh, right.

**Dave**   It's despicable, I know.

*Pause.*

Joanne . . . –

**Joanne**   No, it is despicable, yer right.

**Dave**   I mean . . . –

**Joanne**   D'yer know how long it's took us just to make the minimum payments?

*Pause.*

D'yer know that, Dave, d'yer?

**Dave**   No, I . . . –

**Joanne**   To consolidate each and every one of your fuck-ups so I'm not doped up on pharmaceuticals year on in? D'yer know how long that takes?

*Pause.*

Why d'yer think my dad's still workin' 'is arse off at sixty-fuckin'-five? What else d'yer think that shop's still payin' for, eh?

*Pause.*

D'yer even think about what it takes to admit that yer husband's not comin' home? To stand there like a scrounger and admit that he'd rather be anywhere else but here, with me? Have you any idea what that takes?

*Pause.*

Shall I tell yer how many men I've slept with since you left?

**Dave**   Oh . . . –

**Joanne**   It's not like I 'ant had the choice.

*Pause.*

**Dave**   No, thanks.

*Long pause.*

Thanks, that's . . . –

**Joanne**   Oh, yeah I spent it alright.

**Dave**   What, sorry?

**Joanne**   I spent it because you let me, Dave.

*Pause.*

**Dave**   Oh . . . –

**Joanne**   Because I were too fuckin' young t' know any different, because I still believed . . .

*Pause.*

Because you sat there in the back o' that cab and proposed t' me that night. Some kid with his big soppy eyes starin' up at me – you alone, Dave, it were you, remember? Because it were you who made it seem possible, because you promised me the world, and because I bought into that bollocks too. Because I see your face on every poor drunken cunt, and it's taken us what? It's taken this to admit that we were wrong, to stand accountable even?  After I have to come and beg yer, once I've run out o' fuckin' time?

**Dave**   Of course there's time.

**Joanne**   I don't have that luxury, look at me!

*Long pause.*

Stood there wi' yer Chardonnay and yer endangered fuckin' species.

*She reaches for and lights a cigarette.*

*Long pause.*

**Dave**   Look, Joanne . . . –

**Joanne**   I think yer'd better get yerself cleaned up don't you?

**Dave**   I mean.

*Long pause.*

I mean, if yer'd just let me . . . –

**Joanne**   Clean it up f' fucksake, yer makin' me feel sick.

*Long pause.*

**Dave**   Joanne, please, after everything.

*Pause.*

Can we not just . . . ?

**Joanne**   Viagra.

**Dave**   What?

**Joanne**   I managed to get hold of some Viagra.

*She opens her handbag and rummages inside.*

*Pause.*

(*While rummaging.*) Yer don't have t' look at me like that either, Dave.

**Dave**   No, I'm not.

**Joanne**   Yer've said yer piece already.

*She removes a box or strip of Viagra tablets from her bag.*

*Pause.*

**Dave**   No, that's . . .

**Joanne**   I think a couple should do it.

*Pause.*

Well, go on.

**Dave**   Yeah.

*He takes the Viagra from* **Joanne**.

**Dave**   Yeah, thanks.

*He examines the pills.*

*Pause.*

Thanks, I'll . . .

**Joanne**   That alright for yer?

**Dave**   Course.

**Joanne**   Well then.

**Dave** *doesn't budge.*

*Long pause.*

**Joanne**   Do it, Dave, . . . –

**Dave** (*as he goes*)   I just said so didn't I?

*He exits into the bathroom, shutting the door behind him.*

*He switches the bathroom light on and moves straight to the sink.*

*He places the Viagra tablets on the edge of the sink.*

*He checks his scars in the mirrors on the bathroom cabinet.*

*Pause.*

*He turns on the taps and fills up the sink with hot water, still checking his scars.*

*Once the sink is filled, he turns the taps off.*

*Pause.*

*He hesitates.*

*Pause.*

*He grabs the Viagra tablets and shoves them in his mouth.*

*He fills up the plastic beaker with cold water.*

*He gulps the water and swallows the pills.*

*Pause.*

*He proceeds to wash his face.*

*As he does the above,* **Joanne** *slowly straightens herself out – her clothes, hair, etc.*

*Long pause.*

**Joanne** *pulls herself up off the futon, and moves to the kitchen area.*

*She gulps down some wine from the wine glass.*

*Pause.*

*She hesitates.*

*Pause.*

*She reaches for her cigarettes.*

*Pause.*

*She puts the cigarettes down.*

*She hesitates.*

*Pause.*

*She picks up the CD and takes it out of its case.*

*Pause.*

*She takes the CD, her wine and her cigarettes, and moves to the office area.*

*She sits down.*

*Pause.*

*She switches on the laptop, and places the CD in its compartment.*

*Long pause.*

*She clicks the mouse.*

*Long pause.*

*She clicks the mouse.*

*Long pause.*

*She double-clicks the mouse.*

*Pause.*

*Sam Cooke's 'A Change is Gonna Come' begins to play from the laptop.*

**Joanne** *peers through the blinds, looking out of the window, listening.*

*As she does this . . .*

**Dave** – *washed and dried* – *exits the bathroom, and enters the living space.*

*He hesitates.*

*Pause.*

*He enters the bedroom.*

*Pause.*

*He hesitates.*

*Pause.*

*He moves to the bedside cabinet, and, sitting on the bed, rummages through it.*

*He digs out his chequebook.*

*Pause.*

*He rummages through the cabinet.*

*Pause.*

*He finds a pen.*

*Pause.*

*He writes a cheque.*

*Long pause.*

*He tears the cheque out of the chequebook.*

*Pause.*

*He hesitates.*

*Pause.*

*He stands up and, taking the cheque with him, leaves the bedroom.*

*He moves through the living area and into the kitchen area.*

*Pause.*

*He takes the wine bottle.*

*He fills up the wine glasses with the remaining wine.*

*As he does this . . .*

**Joanne**, *sitting in the office area, turns the music's volume down.*

*Pause.*

*She lights another cigarette.*

*Pause.*

**Dave** *takes one of the wine glasses.*
*Holding the wine glass, and the cheque, he hesitates.*

*Long pause.*

**Dave** *makes to move to* **Joanne**, *when . . .*

**Joanne**    Yer know I was taught t' believe that I could have anything I wanted.

*Pause.*

I was taught t' believe that, Dave.

*Pause.*

I was led t' believe that I could do anything. Be anything.

*Long pause.*

Anything that was out there, anything at all. If I applied myself. If I worked hard enough, I mean. If I was just . . . –

*Pause.*

If I was just fucking able.

*Pause.*

That the world was there for those who fought for it. That there was somethin' yer could call equality. That there were jobs for all, and enough opportunities to not . . .

*Long pause.*

To not have to go through everythin' my own fuckin' mother went through. Compromised n' bound to some idea of what and who you're meant to be. Every single one of 'em, Dave. The centuries of . . .

*Pause.*

And that my generation. That together we might some'ow . . . –

*Pause.*

That I might not 'ave to carry that burden. That my success would change all that, and we'd be the first to really . . .

*Long pause.*

And that with all I achieved.

*Pause.*

That in some small fuckin' way I might just . . .

*Pause.*

Give somethin' back to all them women.

*Pause.*

The women who couldn't fuckin' stand there and . . .

*Pause.*

Who fought so hard for women like me . . . –

*Pause.*

Who could never even dream . . . –

*Pause.*

Who couldn't even contemplate . . . –

*Long pause.*

And then he comes along.

*Pause.*

He always comes along.

*Pause.*

And then yer realise that nothing's fuckin' changed.

*Pause.*

That it's the men who change, not us.

*Pause.*

It's the men who've changed and allowed us our . . .

*Pause.*

And you realise that all these little freedoms.

*Pause.*

That everything comes at a price. That we're not actually equipped . . .

*Pause.*

That yer have to be young and beautiful.

*Pause.*

That not even yer own body lets yer . . .

*Pause.*

And that all yer dreams, all that ambition.

*Pause.*

All yer so-called . . . −

**Dave**   I thought yer had yer own business now.

**Joanne**   What?

**Dave**   The bees. The little bumblebees.

*Long pause.*

**Joanne**   Yeah, well . . . −

**Dave**   I thought yer said.

*Long pause.*

Joanne . . . –

**Joanne**   Well fuck 'em anyway.

**Dave**   Who?

**Joanne**   Fuck 'em all, Dave, yeah.

*Pause.*

Fuck Pankhurst. Fuck Germaine Greer. Fuck Thatcher.

*Pause.*

And fuck *Marie* bastard *Claire* n' all.

*Pause.*

I'll throw the lot of 'em on the fire.

**Dave**   Which fire?

**Joanne**   *Marie Claire.*

**Dave**   Oh . . .

**Joanne**   *Vanity Fair. Elle. Vogue. In Style.*

*Pause.*

I'll burn the lot of 'em, Dave, yeah. Stupid bitches.

*Pause.*

I'll be as fat n' as old n' as ugly as God made me, thanks.

*Long pause.*

I'll happily have his dinner on the table.

**Dave**   Who?

**Joanne**   I'll iron his shirts.

*Pause.*

I'll iron his shirts and his socks. I'll cook his dinner, wash his pots.

*Pause.*

I'd give anything, Dave. Really I would.

*She stubs her cigarette out.*

*Long pause.*

*She peers through the blinds.*

It comes back.

*Long pause.*

I said it comes back.

**Dave**    Sorry, what?

**Joanne**    Yer accent.

**Dave**    Oh . . . –

**Joanne**    When yer get mad. Yer accent creeps back.

**Dave**    Oh, right.

*Long pause.*

**Dave** *puts the cheque and the wine glass down on the kitchen counter.*

*He sits on one of the stools.*

*He sips from his own glass of wine.*

*Long pause.*

**Joanne** *turns away from the blinds and stands.*

*Pause.*

*She moves to the kitchen area.*

*Pause.*

*She takes her glass of wine and sips from it.*

*Pause.*

*She puts her wine glass on the counter, then strokes* **Dave**'s *hair, moving it away from his brow.*

*Long pause.*

**Joanne** *moves behind the counter.*

*She starts clearing up the mess on the kitchen counter – clearing up the chorizo and putting it in the bin, returning the ingredients to the cupboards, washing down the chopping board, straightening up, etc.*

*Long pause.*

**Joanne** (*as she cleans up*)    I mean.

*Pause.*

I mean if there's somethin' . . .

*Pause.*

*She hesitates.*

**Dave** *climbs off the kitchen stool, and* . . .

**Joanne**    I mean, if yer'd really I didn't . . . –

**Dave** *grabs* **Joanne** *from behind.*

**Joanne**    Ow! Jesus Christ! . . . –

**Dave** *pulls down* **Joanne**'s *tracksuit bottoms and underwear.*

**Joanne**    Jesus Christ, Dave.

**Dave** *drags his own trousers and pants down.*

**Joanne**    Dave, please yer don't have to . . . –

**Dave** *fucks* **Joanne** *against the kitchen counter.*

**Joanne**    Alright.

**Dave** *fucks* **Joanne** *against the kitchen counter.*

**Joanne**    Alright, just . . . –

**Dave** *fucks* **Joanne** *against the kitchen counter.*

*Time passes.*

**Dave** *stops, catches his breath.*

*Pause.*

**Dave** *fucks* **Joanne** *against the kitchen counter.*

*Time passes.*

**Dave** *stops, catches his breath.*

*Pause.*

**Joanne** *helps* **Dave**, *reaching between their legs, and guiding his penis.*

**Dave** *fucks* **Joanne** *against the kitchen counter.*

*A long time passes.*

**Dave** *stops, catches his breath.*

*Long pause.*

**Dave** *pulls up his trousers and pants.*

*He grabs his glass of wine, and marches to the bedroom.*

*He enters the bedroom, slamming the door behind him.*

*He sits on the bed.*

*Long pause.*

**Joanne** *pulls up her underwear and tracksuit bottoms.*

*Long pause.*

*She sips her wine.*

*Pause.*

*She hesitates.*

*Pause.*

*She moves across the living space and stops by the bedroom door.*

*Pause.*

*She knocks lightly on the bedroom door.*

**Joanne**   Dave . . . –

**Dave**  (*from the bedroom*)   Look, I'm sorry, alright?

**Joanne**   I think yer meant t' give 'em an hour at least.

**Dave** (*from the bedroom*)   No, that's . . .

*Pause.*

Thanks.

*Pause.*

Thanks, I'll bear that in mind.

**Joanne** *opens the bedroom door and enters.*

**Joanne** (*as she enters*)   Yer don't have to lock yerself away.

**Dave**   No, really . . . –

**Joanne**   I'm happy to wait.

**Dave**   Eh?

**Joanne**   I'm happy to wait with yer, Dave.

**Dave**   Oh . . .

**Joanne**   It's not a problem.

*She sits on the bed, next to* **Dave**.

*Very long pause.*

**Joanne**   I could get used t' this place.

**Dave**   Could yer?

*Long pause.*

Yeah, well . . . –

**Joanne**   Stupid old cunt.

**Dave**   No, that's . . .

*Very long pause.*

Thought of any names yet?

**Joanne**   Sorry?

**Dave**   Any names?

*Very long pause.*

**Joanne** *gets up off the bed, and moves to the bedroom window.*

*She opens the blinds.*

*Pause.*

*She peers through the window.*

*Pause.*

*She grabs the window and wrenches it open.*

*The noise of the streets below.*

*She leans out of the window, looking out at the opposite flats.*

*Long pause.*

**Dave** *puts his wine down, and stands.*

*He moves across to* **Joanne**, *standing behind her.*

**Dave** *and* **Joanne** *look out the window.*

*Very long pause.*

**Dave** *puts his hand round* **Joanne**'s *waist.*

*Lights fade.*

# Methuen Drama Student Editions

Jean Anouilh *Antigone* • John Arden *Serjeant Musgrave's Dance*
Alan Ayckbourn *Confusions* • Aphra Behn *The Rover*
Edward Bond *Lear* • Bertolt Brecht *The Caucasian Chalk Circle*
*Life of Galileo* • *Mother Courage and her Children*
*The Resistible Rise of Arturo Ui* • *The Threepenny Opera*
Anton Chekhov *The Cherry Orchard* • *The Seagull* • *Three Sisters*
*Uncle Vanya* • Caryl Churchill *Serious Money* • *Top Girls*
Shelagh Delaney *A Taste of Honey* • Euripides *Elektra* • *Medea*
Dario Fo *Accidental Death of an Anarchist* • Michael Frayn *Copenhagen*
John Galsworthy *Strife* • Nikolai Gogol *The Government Inspector*
Robert Holman *Across Oka* • Henrik Ibsen *A Doll's House* • *Ghosts*
*Hedda Gabler* • Charlotte Keatley *My Mother Said I Never Should*
Bernard Kops *Dreams of Anne Frank* • Federico García Lorca
*Blood Wedding* • *Doña Rosita the Spinster* (bilingual edition) • *The House
of Bernarda Alba* • (bilingual edition) • *Yerma* (bilingual edition) • David
Mamet *Glengarry Glen Ross* • *Oleanna* • Patrick Marber *Closer* • John
Marston *The Malcontent* • Joe Orton *Loot* • Luigi Pirandello *Six
Characters in Search of an Author* • Mark Ravenhill *Shopping and
F\*\*\*ing* • Willy Russell *Blood Brothers* • *Educating Rita* • Sophocles
*Antigone* • *Oedipus the King* • Wole Soyinka *Death and the King's
Horseman* • August Strindberg *Miss Julie* • J. M. Synge *The Playboy
of the Western World* • Theatre Workshop *Oh What a Lovely War*
Timberlake Wertenbaker *Our Country's Good* • Arnold Wesker *The
Merchant* • Oscar Wilde *The Importance of Being Earnest* • Tennessee
Williams *A Streetcar Named Desire* • *The Glass Menagerie*

## Methuen Drama Modern Plays

*include work by*

Edward Albee
Jean Anouilh
John Arden
Margaretta D'Arcy
Peter Barnes
Sebastian Barry
Brendan Behan
Dermot Bolger
Edward Bond
Bertolt Brecht
Howard Brenton
Anthony Burgess
Simon Burke
Jim Cartwright
Caryl Churchill
Noël Coward
Lucinda Coxon
Sarah Daniels
Nick Darke
Nick Dear
Shelagh Delaney
David Edgar
David Eldridge
Dario Fo
Michael Frayn
John Godber
Paul Godfrey
David Greig
John Guare
Peter Handke
David Harrower
Jonathan Harvey
Iain Heggie
Declan Hughes
Terry Johnson
Sarah Kane
Charlotte Keatley
Barrie Keeffe
Howard Korder

Robert Lepage
Doug Lucie
Martin McDonagh
John McGrath
Terrence McNally
David Mamet
Patrick Marber
Arthur Miller
Mtwa, Ngema & Simon
Tom Murphy
Phyllis Nagy
Peter Nichols
Sean O'Brien
Joseph O'Connor
Joe Orton
Louise Page
Joe Penhall
Luigi Pirandello
Stephen Poliakoff
Franca Rame
Mark Ravenhill
Philip Ridley
Reginald Rose
Willy Russell
Jean-Paul Sartre
Sam Shepard
Wole Soyinka
Simon Stephens
Shelagh Stephenson
Peter Straughan
C. P. Taylor
Theatre de Complicite
Theatre Workshop
Sue Townsend
Judy Upton
Timberlake Wertenbaker
Roy Williams
Snoo Wilson
Victoria Wood

## Methuen Drama Contemporary Dramatists

*include*

John Arden (two volumes)
Arden & D'Arcy
Peter Barnes (three volumes)
Sebastian Barry
Dermot Bolger
Edward Bond (eight volumes)
Howard Brenton
  (two volumes)
Richard Cameron
Jim Cartwright
Caryl Churchill
  (two volumes)
Sarah Daniels (two volumes)
Nick Darke
David Edgar (three volumes)
David Eldridge
Ben Elton
Dario Fo (two volumes)
Michael Frayn (three volumes)
John Godber (three volumes)
Paul Godfrey
David Greig
John Guare
Lee Hall (two volumes)
Peter Handke
Jonathan Harvey
  (two volumes)
Declan Hughes
Terry Johnson (three volumes)
Sarah Kane
Barrie Keeffe
Bernard-Marie Koltès
  (two volumes)
David Lan
Bryony Lavery
Deborah Levy
Doug Lucie

David Mamet (four volumes)
Martin McDonagh
Duncan McLean
Anthony Minghella
  (two volumes)
Tom Murphy (five volumes)
Phyllis Nagy
Anthony Neilson
Philip Osment
Gary Owen
Louise Page
Stewart Parker (two volumes)
Joe Penhall
Stephen Poliakoff
  (three volumes)
David Rabe
Mark Ravenhill
Christina Reid
Philip Ridley
Willy Russell
Eric-Emmanuel Schmitt
Ntozake Shange
Sam Shepard (two volumes)
Wole Soyinka (two volumes)
Simon Stephens
Shelagh Stephenson
David Storey (three volumes)
Sue Townsend
Judy Upton
Michel Vinaver
  (two volumes)
Arnold Wesker (two volumes)
Michael Wilcox
Roy Williams (two volumes)
Snoo Wilson (two volumes)
David Wood (two volumes)
Victoria Wood

## Methuen Drama World Classics

*include*

Jean Anouilh (two volumes)
Brendan Behan
Aphra Behn
Bertolt Brecht (eight volumes)
Büchner
Bulgakov
Calderón
Čapek
Anton Chekhov
Noël Coward (eight volumes)
Feydeau
Eduardo De Filippo
Max Frisch
John Galsworthy
Gogol
Gorky (two volumes)
Harley Granville Barker
    (two volumes)
Victor Hugo
Henrik Ibsen (six volumes)
Jarry

Lorca (three volumes)
Marivaux
Mustapha Matura
David Mercer (two volumes)
Arthur Miller (five volumes)
Molière
Musset
Peter Nichols (two volumes)
Joe Orton
A. W. Pinero
Luigi Pirandello
Terence Rattigan
    (two volumes)
W. Somerset Maugham
    (two volumes)
August Strindberg
    (three volumes)
J. M. Synge
Ramón del Valle-Inclan
Frank Wedekind
Oscar Wilde